THE

WISDOM OF EGYPT

AND THE

OLD TESTAMENT IN THE LIGHT

OF THE

NEWLY DISCOVERED TEACHINGS

OF

AMEN-EM-OPE

(1927)

W. O. E. Oesterley

ISBN 0-7661-0445-1

Kessinger Publishing's Rare Reprints
Thousands of Scarce and Hard-to-Find Books!

·   ·   ·
·   ·   ·
·   ·   ·
·   ·   ·
·   ·   ·
·   ·   ·
·   ·   ·
·   ·   ·
·   ·   ·
·   ·   ·
·   ·   ·
·   ·   ·
·   ·   ·
·   ·   ·
·   ·   ·
·   ·   ·
·   ·   ·
·   ·   ·
·   ·   ·
·   ·   ·

THE WISDOM OF EGYPT
& THE OLD TESTAMENT

IN THE LIGHT OF THE NEWLY DISCOVERED
'TEACHING OF AMEN-EM-OPE'

BY

W. O. E. OESTERLEY, D.D.

PROFESSOR OF HEBREW AND OLD TESTAMENT EXEGESIS
KING'S COLLEGE, UNIVERSITY OF LONDON

LONDON
SOCIETY FOR PROMOTING
CHRISTIAN   KNOWLEDGE
NEW YORK AND TORONTO : THE MACMILLAN CO.
1927

Printed in Great Britain

PREFACE

THE following chapters are written for the general reader who may be interested in the recently published remarkable Egyptian Wisdom book called the 'Teaching of Amen-em-ope,' and its relation to some of the Old Testament writings.

The present book is the expansion of a paper read before the Society for Old Testament Study, and an article in the *Zeitschrift für die alttestamentliche Wissenschaft*. The writer soon came to feel that the usually accepted opinion that the 'Teaching of Amen-em-ope' was one of the sources utilised by the compiler of the Book of Proverbs and nothing more called for some modification; and more especially that the religious standpoint of the former, which in some important respects agreed with the religion of Israel, deserved more attention than it had yet received.

The first chapter is introductory and deals with what has so far been written about Amen-em-ope's book. Chapter II discusses in some detail the religious standpoint of the writer, Amen-em-ope, from which it is concluded that there is affinity between his religious and ethical ideas and those of some of the Old Testament writings.

But before this is further considered, and illustrated by means of detailed comparison, a chapter is devoted to a brief enumeration of the historical periods during which Israel and Egypt came into close contact, in order to ascertain the times at which the influence of one upon the other might be likely to have been exercised. Chapters IV and V are devoted respectively to a comparison between the ' Teaching of Amen-em-ope ' and the Book of Proverbs, and to other Old Testament passages in other books, especially Deuteronomy and the Psalms. Some concluding considerations are contained in the last chapter.

The writer's primary interest is in the Old Testament and the religion of Israel ; he is no Egyptologist, and has therefore to rely for quotations from the Egyptian book on the translations which have been published ; these are enumerated in Chapter I, § 1. He had completed the unpretending little work when he heard that Professor F. Ll. Griffith was about to publish a new translation. By an act of kindness, which it is difficult to acknowledge adequately, Professor Griffith sent the writer a proof-copy of this translation, with permission to make full use of it. This was a great boon, and an expression of warm gratitude is herewith tendered to Professor Griffith. The reasons why his translation transcends all the others hitherto published in importance will be seen on pp. 2 ff. But Professor Griffith's kindness did not end with this ; he also read through the whole of the type-written copy of these pages and made a number of corrections where the translation of passages was faulty or ambiguous and the interpretation questionable ; his help has been invaluable, and is sincerely appreciated. The writer has also to express his sincere thanks to the Oriel Professor, Canon D. C. Simpson, for his kindness in letting him see a proof-copy of an article, appended to that of Professor Griffith, on the relation between the Egyptian book and the Book of Proverbs. And, finally, the writer wishes to utter a word of hearty thanks to Professor Gressmann, of Berlin, for reading through the type-written copy of the following pages and for giving some very valuable suggestions, all of which have been adopted.

CONTENTS

CONTENTS

THE WISDOM OF EGYPT
AND THE OLD TESTAMENT

CHAPTER I

THE 'TEACHING OF AMEN-EM-OPE'

I. *Literature*

THE full text of the ' Teaching of Amen-em-ope ' was first published by Sir Ernest Wallis Budge in *Facsimiles of Egyptian Hieratic Papyri in the British Museum,* Second Series, pp. 9-18, 41–51, Plates i.–xiv. (1923) ; these plates contain the whole of the text photographed. The same writer has also published *The Teaching of Amen-em-Apt, the son of Kanekht* (1924) ; in this volume the author gives an English translation with notes, together with an elaborate account of the contents and teaching of the Egyptian book ; a transcription of the original text is also given. Dr. H. O. Lange published in 1925 *Das Weisheitsbuch des Amen-em-ope* ; this is a valuable book, containing the text, a German translation, and commentary.

Another German translation with brief notes has also been published by Ranke in Gressmann's *Altorientalische Texte zum Alten Testament,* pp. 38 ff. (1926). Besides these volumes the following important articles have appeared in various publications :

Lange, a translation of the text in the *Nordisk Tidskrift* (1924) ; Erman, *Das Weisheitsbuch des*

Amen-em-ope, in the *Orientalistische Literatur-Zeitung*, cols. 241–252 (1924). This is a revision of Lange's translation just mentioned. The same writer, *Eine Ägyptische Quelle der Sprüche Salomos*, in the *Sitzungsberichte der preussischen Akademie der Wissenschaften*, Philosophisch-historische Klasse, xv., xvi. (May 1924) ; Sellin, in the *Deutsche Literaturzeitung*, xvii., xxvi. (1924) ; Gressmann, *Die neugefundene Lehre des Amen-em-ope und die vorexilische Spruchdichtung Israels*, in the *Zeitschrift für die alttestamentliche Wissenschaft*, pp. 272 ff. (1924) ; this is a very important article for the student of the Old Testament ; the translation of the Egyptian text is confined to those passages which bear on the Book of Proverbs ; it is Erman's translation, modified here and there by Sethe. Further, Grimme has written in the *Orientalistische Literatur-Zeitung*, cols. 57–62 (1925), and Löhr in the same journal, cols. 72–73 (1925) ; Sethe, *Der Mensch denkt, Gott lenkt bei den alten Ägyptern*, in *Nachrichten der Gesellschaft der Wissenschaften zu Göttingen*, Philologisch-historische Klasse, pp. 141 ff. (1926) ; S. A. B. Mercer, *A New Found Book of Proverbs*, in the *Anglican Theological Review* (Jan. 1926) ; Sethe, in the *Zeitschrift für Ägyptische Sprache*, lxii. (1926) ; Ludwig Keimer, in the *American Journal of Semitic Languages and Literature* (Oct. 1926).

The most recent and at the same time the most valuable piece of work on the subject is the article published by Prof. Griffith in *The Journal of Egyptian Archaeology*, ' The Teaching of Amenophis, the son of Kanekht ' (xii. pp. 191 ff., 1926). It will be well to quote some words of the writer, from which it will be seen how important this latest piece of work on the subject is : ' It is now time that an English translation, embodying all the new readings and interpretations, should be attempted. Towards its accomplishment I have had not only the printed works . . . to consult.

In 1924 Professor Erman transcribed and translated the whole text on slips for the great hieroglyphic dictionary which is being prepared at Berlin, and of these he most kindly sent me a complete copy. Moreover, Dr. Lange had no personal access to the original by which the evidence of the facsimile could be checked, though Dr. Gardiner verified some readings for him. By the kindness of Dr. Hall I have had ample facilities for examining the papyrus, and have thus been put into a position of great advantage for verifying old readings and obtaining new ones in doubtful cases ; this was very important in view of certain imperfections in the facsimile mentioned below. I have used the whole text at Oxford in a Seminar-class which Dr. Blackman was good enough to attend, and have therefore had the benefit of his valuable suggestions ; and Dr. Gardiner has given me an exact copy of his careful transcript, made many years ago, of the Turin tablet. At the last moment Prof. Sethe, Erman's successor at Berlin, has sent me some very important notes which he has published, or is about to publish.' [1]

The imperfections in the facsimile referred to arise from the fact that ' where the papyrus had been torn strips of transparent paper had been laid on in such a way as to cover written portions as well as unwritten ; in these places the writing can be seen by the eye without much difficulty, but the photographing lens has too often failed entirely to penetrate the paper, so that the writing appears to cease in the facsimile where the paper begins. In another place a tear across the page has been ill-adjusted so that the gaps resulting appear as black lines in the facsimile and have led to misreadings.'

Prof. Griffith's article is followed by one by Canon D. C. Simpson, ' The Hebrew Book of Proverbs and the Teaching of Amenophis.' This deals only with

[1] *Op. cit.*, p. 192.

those passages in the Egyptian writing which bear on
the Book of Proverbs ; but it is a learned and valuable
piece of work, and is of special importance for the study
of the Hebrew text of Proverbs, so far as the passages
dealt with are concerned. Prof. Simpson draws
attention, however, to the fact that the resemblances
between the Egyptian writing and the Book of Proverbs
are not the only marks of relationship which the former
seems to have with the Old Testament. This fact will
be further dealt with in the following pages.

II. *The ' Teaching of Amen-em-ope '*

The Egyptian text of this work is contained in
a hieratic papyrus, numbered 10474, in the British
Museum. It is ' one of the numerous treasures which
Sir Ernest Budge brought home for the British Museum
in 1888 from his first Mission to Egypt.' [1] It came
from Akhmim, the ancient Panopolis, in Upper Egypt.
The length of the papyrus is 12 ft. $1\frac{1}{2}$ in., and it is
10 inches in breadth at the widest part.

The text, of which there are twenty-seven columns,
is a copy made by a scribe named Senu of the work
which in the papyrus is entitled, ' Teaching how to
live.'

The work was evidently held in high estimation,
and it must at one time have enjoyed a wide circula-
tion, since it was used as a school-book, as is shown
by an ancient wooden Egyptian writing-tablet preserved in the Museum at Turin ; on this tablet a school-
boy copied out daily four or five verses from the
Teaching.[2]

[1] Griffith, *op. cit.*, p. 191.
[2] The tablet contains thirty-two lines from Amen-em-ope ; the
writer has noted in the margin the amount he copied out for his
daily portion. See Erman, *Sitzungsberichte* . . . p. 86 ; Lange, *Das
Weisheitsbuch*, p. 9 ; Griffith, *op. cit.*, p. 193.

The work was composed by an Egyptian sage named Amen-em-ope,[1] the son of Ka-Nakht. He was 'in charge of the land and of corn,' but whether for the whole of Egypt or for a district only does not appear. He clearly belonged to the region of Panopolis and Abydos, which lie opposite each other along the Nile ; in each of these cities he possessed a sepulchral monument, and he probably had been a pious benefactor to their temples.[2] His work is referred to as the fruit [3] of a scribe of Egypt (Preface i. 14), as though implying that it was not borrowed ; that this should be mentioned is interesting, for it raises the question as to whether there is anything in the work which might suggest the idea of borrowing. The subject will come before us again.

The text of the copy of his work is, upon the whole, good, according to the experts, though it has blemishes. ' The length of the text adds to its importance, for no other document of its class now known contains so many unmutilated lines.' [4] Ranke points out that the copyist who wrote this text has probably been somewhat careless in parts, and did not appear to have understood the text of some passages.[5] Lange speaks of the writing as regular, in general, and clear, being evidently the handiwork of a practised scribe ; but he says that the text has many mistakes, omissions, wrong signs, and misunderstandings on the part of the scribe.[6] Sethe likewise says that there is much verbal corruption, and that there are still many problems

---

[1] The name is written differently by different scholars ; Wallis Budge transcribes it Amen-em-Apt ; German Egyptologists write it Amen-em-ope ; Griffith adopts the Greek form Amenophis. The name occurs on the Amarna tablets in the form Aman-appa (Ranke, p. 38).

[2] Griffith, op. cit., pp. 196–198 and 226 f.

[3] Prof. Griffith believes that the word in the original will bear the sense of ' intellectual fruit ' (in a private communication).

[4] Wallis Budge, op. cit., p. 101.

[5] Op. cit., p. 38.   [6] Das Weisheitsbuch . . ., pp. 8, 9.

to be solved.[1]   Griffith, too, says that the text bristles
with difficulties,[2] and this is amply borne out by reading
his detailed commentary, as well as that of Lange.

The former says in his article in the *Journal of
Egyptian Archaeology* : 'Translation of the text of
Amenophis is especially difficult for several reasons,
and much of the version that follows is still only pro-
visional. The mode of expression is artificial, using
rare and poetical words and idioms ; the phraseology
is concise, employing few periphrases to clarify the
grammatical connexions ; the sentences are short and
disconnected ; the spelling of words is inexact and
unetymological to a degree unusual even in such late
texts ; and, lastly, more than one clear instance of
scribal error in this portion of the papyrus, for which
there exists the parallel text of the Turin tablet, itself
very faulty, shows that the student has to reckon with
the probability of many errors elsewhere ' (p. 193).

There are other difficulties which this copy of
Amen-em-ope's work present. The exact meaning of
many of the words used is unknown, and is not to be
found in the existing dictionaries. Lange remarks on
the not inconsiderable number of new and unknown
words which is one of the chief difficulties in the way
of understanding some parts. Gardiner says that the
work is written in a ' quite peculiar orthography.' [3]

And then there is the further difficulty which occurs
in quite a number of passages, even where the text is
clear enough, of getting at the author's meaning. The
variety of interpretations on the part of experts
illustrates this. Lange confesses in the Preface to his
book that there is much in the thought of Amen-em-ope
which he does not understand, and that he finds it
impossible to explain some passages.

[1] *Der Mensch denkt* . . ., p. 141.
[2] In private conversation.
[3] In a letter to the present writer.

But while the existence of these difficulties is realised, it must not be thought that they constitute a bar to the general understanding of the work ; they only apply to what are, after all, exceptional passages or to details. The meaning of the great bulk of the book is clear. In comparing the various translations which have been made of the whole or parts of the work, one cannot fail to be struck by the agreement in the general sense of passages ; there may be variety of opinion on details ; but apart from a certain number of exceptions there is much consensus of opinion among expert Egyptologists.[1]

The work, which is written in Neo-Egyptian, is composed in ' chosen and elegant ' language (Lange), containing apt comparisons and many poetical turns. It consists of thirty chapters [2] (lit. ' houses '), each containing a varying number of proverbs. Many of these are short and pithy, while other passages take the form of a miniature essay. But structurally the whole is written in poetical form, being divided strophically ; Lange says that there is no kind of doubt about this, most of the strophes consisting of four lines, some of two only.[3]

The Egyptian character of the work is very pronounced throughout. This is to be observed in the kind of mental pictures drawn, in the thoughts, and the way in which they are expressed, in the various implications, in the mention of Egyptian gods, as well as in the references to external things, customs, social conditions and the like. Notable illustrations are the references to the Nile and Nilotic boat-work.

---

[1] Wallis Budge's translation is an exception ; but since his book was published the text has been subjected to much scrutiny and study by other experts, Erman, Ranke, Lange, Sethe, Griffith, and others.

[2] The number thirty is, according to Sethe, taken from the thirty days of the calendar month.

[3] *Op. cit.*, pp. 10, 11 ; see also Griffith, *op. cit.*, p. 227.

III. *Date of the Work*

It cannot yet be said with certainty what even the approximate date of this work is. The opinions of experts differ considerably; but the weight of argument seems to favour a relatively late date. Wallis Budge thinks it highly probable that Amen-em-ope was born during one of the reigns of the kings of the XVIII dynasty,[1] and assigns his work to the first half of this period, 'probably soon after Amenhotep I had rebuilt and endowed the priesthood of Amen.'[2] The British Museum papyrus he judges by the general style of the writing to have been made under the XX or XXI dynasty. He would thus date the work itself about the middle of the fifteenth or sixteenth century B.C., and the copy of it roughly 1200–1000 B.C. Erman, who is followed by Ranke, thinks that the papyrus belongs to the tenth century B.C., but is perhaps 'considerably later.' Lange and Griffith have gone into the question of the date more thoroughly than anyone else at present; the former says that the work is written in a variety of the Neo-Egyptian language which cannot be earlier than the XXII dynasty, and thinks that it is much later.[3] He points to the use of various words the occurrence of which is not attested before Persian or Greek times; he mentions also the form of a certain preposition always used in the work, but which is only used from the Persian period onwards (sixth to fourth century B.C.)[4]; a number of the signs have forms which first appear in the fourth century B.C.; and the writing of one verse to a line points to a late date for the papyrus, the earlier method being to separate the verses with a red dot.[5] He says, further, that if one com-

---

[1] The duration of this dynasty was approximately 1580–1350 B.C.
[2] *Op. cit.*, p. 96.   [3] *Op. cit.*, p. 14.
[4] *Op. cit.*, p. 41.   [5] *Op. cit.*, p. 8.

pares the writing of the papyrus of Nes-min, belonging to the year 312–311 B.C., with our papyrus, one sees that the differences are not at all great.[1]

Professor Griffith also assigns the papyrus to a comparatively late date, placing it in the time of the XXVI dynasty (seventh to sixth century B.C.). In a private letter to the present writer he says : ' The date is a very difficult matter to settle, impossible at present ; but some of Lange's instances of spelling " first found in the Greek period " can be put back much earlier—to the time of Tirhaka,[2] chiefly from unpublished material. I am inclined to date the text about 600 B.C.' In his article he says, in reference to the names which occur in the body of the work, that they ' give us singularly little help in determining the date of the composition. They conduct us at once to a period not earlier than the XVIII dynasty,[3] but leave us in doubt thereafter, although collectively they give the impression of a later date, say XXI to XXVI [5] dynasty. It is, of course, conceivable that the names are fictitious.' Then with regard to the British Museum papyrus containing the copy of the work he says : ' The names of the writer of the papyrus, Senu, and of his father Pemū, in the colophon are helpful, for Pemū appears first late in the XXII dynasty,[6] and is common thereafter to Ptolemaic times,[7] while the only other instance known of Senu is Ptolemaic (Senusheps). On the whole it

---

[1] *Op. cit.*, p. 8.

[2] ' The Biblical Tirhakah (2 Kings xix. 9 = Isa. xxxvii. 9), who reigned, according to a *stele* of the Serapeum, twenty-six complete years ; according to Assyrian sources he died in 668–667 ; consequently his accession to the throne was in 694–693 B.C.' (Müller, in the *Encycl. Bibl.* iv. 5099).

[3] Approximately 1600–1350 B.C.

[4] The Tanite Dynasty, about 1100–945 B.C.

[5] The Saite Dynasty, founded by Psammetichus 660 B.C.

[6] The Libyan Dynasty, founded by Sheshonk I (Shishak in 1 Kings xi. 40, in 945 B.C.).

[7] About 300 B.C. onwards.

may be said that the script and the orthography of the papyrus seem to take us (as far as our present evidence goes) to the XXV dynasty [1] as the earliest date, and the reign of Darius [2] as the latest.' [3]

It will, therefore, be seen that while uncertainty must exist when there are these differences of opinion among experts, the weight of definite evidence points to a date later than the eighth century B.C. rather than before it ; and the possibility must be reckoned with of the work having been composed later still. But however late the date may be, it is not only possible, but probable, that the writer's work included compiling as well as composing ; and that he made use of earlier material may be taken as certain. That Amen-em-ope quotes well-known proverbs in his book (*e.g.* in XVII., XXIII., XXVI.) is evident, as Lange has shown [4] ; and when we come to consider the religious teaching of his book, it is hoped that evidence may be forthcoming which will support the view that he was strongly affected by outside influence. This must, to some extent, have a bearing on the question of date.

In the references to Amen-em-ope's book given in the following pages the large Roman numerals refer to the chapters into which the book is divided, the small Roman numerals indicate the columns of the original MS., and the Arabic numerals refer to the lines.

[1] The Ethiopian Dynasty, founded by Shabaka about 750 B.C.
[2] Darius I reigned from 521–485 B.C.
[3] *Op. cit.*, p. 226.
[4] See his commentary in *Das Weisheitsbuch* . . ., passim.

CHAPTER II

I. *The Religious Spirit of the Book*

IT has been pointed out that Egyptologists are agreed as to the unique character of our book within the whole range of Egyptian literature, so far as this is at present known. This uniqueness centres in the *religious and ethical standpoint* of Amen-em-ope.[1] In the Preface to his book he says he was a scribe (cp. Chap. XV.) ; that he was a sage goes without saying. This is an interesting combination, for we find something approximating to it in Israel. Ezra was a priest and a scribe ; Ben-Sira was a sage and a scribe ; and they were assuredly but representative of many. As a priestly Wisdom-scribe, therefore, Amen-em-ope corresponded to a type of sage which existed in Israel ; and in common with such he was deeply imbued with the religious spirit. In this respect Amen-em-ope's book differs essentially from the other ethical and didactic writings of ancient Egypt which are known to us.[2] ' Not only,' says Lange, ' do we find a whole series of purely religious utterances, but the background of the reflections and exhortations is throughout religious, and religious motives are emphasised again and again.'

[1] To a slight extent a religious atmosphere is to be observed in the *Teaching of Meri-ke-re* (see Erman, *Die Literatur der Aegypter*, pp. 109–119), but it is *very* slight as compared with that in the *Teaching of Amen-em-ope.*

[2] Lange, *op. cit.*, p. 16.

Particularly important is the fact, upon which Lange lays stress, that the writer's religious standpoint 'is singular and noteworthy when one compares it with the " religiosity " which we find expressed or suggested, both as regards the conception of the deity as well as in reference to personal relationship to God, elsewhere in Egyptian literature.'[1] Griffith, too, remarks that the writer sets up ' a higher standard of morality than his predecessors that are known to us had done . . . in other Egyptian teachings the practical quite overshadows the spiritual, but in Amenophis's teaching religion and morality are the chief motives.'[2]

II. *Amen-em-ope's Conception of God*

Although Amen-em-ope makes mention of several of the gods of Egypt—Thoth (XVI.), the two holy animals, the Ibis and the Ape (Baboon) (XV.) by which he was symbolised ; the moon-god (II., VI.) ; Re, the sun-god (V., VII., IX., XVII., XXVI., XXVII.) ; Khnum (IX.) ; and the deities, god and goddess, of Destiny, Shay and Renent (VII., XX.)—yet one gains the impression that these represent manifestations of one God rather than individual realities in the mind of the writer ; in his frequent mention of the deity, he speaks interchangeably of ' the God,' or ' God ' without the article, though Griffith thinks this is mere phraseology without difference of meaning.[3] Lange says that the writer's religious views are usually expressed in an entirely monotheistic direction ; see also Griffith, *op. cit.*, p. 230.

By this it is not meant to say that Amen-em-ope was a monotheist, for, as already pointed out, he

---

[1] *Op. cit.*, p. 17.   [2] *Op. cit.*, p. 227.
[3] A similar thing occurs in other Egyptian writings.

mentions half a dozen Egyptian gods of whose functions he also speaks ; but there can be no doubt that his thoughts tended in a monotheistic direction. The ingrained belief in many gods with their various special characteristics would naturally be apt to cling even though the reasons for that belief had lost their force. Amen-em-ope's use of the expression 'All-ruler' or 'Universal Lord,' in reference to God, shows that he believed in a deity who was above all other gods ; and though this expression occurs in other Egyptian writings, it is indubitable from his whole conception of God that the expression connoted more in his mind than in the minds of others. We shall, therefore, in giving illustrations from his book on this subject, write ' God ' where the deity is mentioned, whether with or without the article ; where the name of a god occurs, Thoth, Re, etc. (which is, however, exceptional), that name will be given. In other Egyptian writings, it is true, ' God ' is also at times used in place of the ordinary gods, but ' Amen-em-ope's religious conception is a much profounder one and enters more deeply into his whole world of thought. . . . To the other Wisdom-teachers piety is a virtue, the thought of death and eternity a motive for right living ; for them God is one who gives wealth and prosperity. But for Amen-em-ope it is the appre-hension of God which determines his conception of life, and his entire conduct of life.' [1]

This high estimate of Amen-em-ope's conception of God is no exaggeration, as will be seen ; and when, added to this, we find a very exalted idea of duty as between man and man, we may well contemplate the possibility of Amen-em-ope's thought having been affected, and indeed infected, by extra-Egyptian influences.

But let us first set before ourselves in some detail

[1] Lange, *op. cit.*, p. 18.

Amen-em-ope's conception of God, as portrayed in his book.

God alone is perfect, and in His sight nothing that is imperfect can subsist (XVIII. xix. 22 ff.). He is the Creator of man, and determines the lot of man (cp. on this VII. x. 12–15) ; some men He exalts, others He brings low ; death and life are in His hands,[1] and all things are according to His will (XXV. xxiv. 13–18). Man proposes, but God disposes ; the future is in His sight, and He alone knows what the morrow will bring forth ; God is the Pilot of the ship (XVIII. xix. 14–17 ; xx. 3 ff.). It is very interesting to observe, too, how Amen-em-ope insists on the divine attribute of righteousness, or justice ; God is the possessor of righteousness, which He imparts to whom He will ; in Chap. XX. xxi. 5, 6, it is said :

Righteousness is the great gift of God, and He giveth it to whom He will.

As a righteous God, sin in any and every form is an abomination to Him, and the evil deeds of men cannot escape His all-seeing eye (XV. xvii. 10–12 ; XVII. xviii. 23 ; xix. 1 ff.). In His sight there is no man without sin, and it is useless to attempt to conceal [2] sin from Him, for ' it is sealed with His finger,' *i.e.* with Him lies the decision as to what is or is not sin, and He will punish it (XVIII. xix. 20, 21). Hypocrisy and lying are an abomination to God, and, above all, one who is double-tongued is hateful to Him (X. xiv. 2, 3). To interfere with the course of justice is to frustrate the divine plans (XX. xxi. 13, 14) ; false oaths are sinful (XI. xiv. 9, 10) ; dishonesty of every kind is detestable to God (*passim*). He punishes the

---

[1] This is presumably what is meant by the phrase : ' He destroyeth and buildeth up daily.'

[2] This seems to be the meaning demanded by the context, but it is only a guess ; the experts all differ in their renderings to some degree. See further on the passage below, p. 50.

passionate man (III. v. 15–17). The possessions of a man are valueless if it involves a transgression against God (XVI. xviii. 10, 11) ; let a man beware of neglecting the guidance of God (XXIV. xxiv. 4, 5) ; the evil-doer will receive punishment (*passim*) ; it is well to have a good conscience (XIII. xvi. 9, 10 ; XVIII. xix. 11, 12). Further, Amen-em-ope is insistent on those things which are pleasing in the sight of God. He blesses just dealing :

> Better is a bushel which God giveth thee
> Than five thousand wrongly gained (VI. viii. 19, 20) ;

and poverty with godliness :

> Better is poverty in the hand of God
> Than wealth in the storehouse.   (VI. ix. 5, 6.)

In XXVIII. xxvi. 13, 14 it is said :

> God loveth him who rejoiceth the meek
> More than him who honoureth the noble.

Griffith renders this a little differently, though the meaning is essentially the same :

> God loveth the happiness of the humble
> More than that the noble be honoured.

The humble in spirit are implicitly commended (XVIII. xix. 22–xx. 2 ; cp. XX. xxi. 15).

In II. v. 7, 8 it is said :

> Another thing good in the heart of God
> Is to pause before speaking.[1]

God upholds him in whom tongue and heart are in accord (X. xiii. 17).

But the passages are more numerous in which virtues are commended and warnings against immoral action are uttered ; for the whole religious outlook of Amen-em-ope shows that, without specifically saying so, he

---

[1] Griffith's rendering.

regards the former as well-pleasing to God, the latter as sinful in His sight, and therefore abhorrent to Him. Thus, truthfulness is commended (XIX. xx. 14) ; consideration in taxing the poor is enjoined, *i.e.* mercy (XIII. xvi. 5–7) ; the need of honesty of purpose in a scribe is insisted upon (XV. xvii. 11–14) ; and in Chap. XIV. there is an exhortation to be independent, and not to be beholden to others and lose one's self-respect by taking gifts from them. The judge is called upon to deal justly, and to deliver property to its rightful owner (XX. xx. 21, 22 ; xxi. 17) ; and in the same connexion it is said :

> Receive no bribe from one who is powerful,
> And oppress not the poor for his benefit.
> (XX. xxi. 3, 4.)

Warnings are uttered against covetousness (XI. xiv. 5, 6 ; XII. xv. 9, 10), against bearing false witness (XIII. xvi. 1), against consorting with evil men (XII. xv. 13, 14 ; XVI. xviii. 6, 7), against bribery (XVII. xix. 4), against dishonesty (XVI. xvii. 18, 19), and against hypocrisy (X. xiii. 13–16).

The religious spirit which permeates his writing shows that in all these things the thought of God is at the back of Amen-em-ope's mind. That he had a real sense of sin is seen from the passage (referred to above) in XVIII. xix. 18–21 :

> Say not, ' I have no sin,'
> And be not at pains to (conceal it ?) ; [1]
> Sin belongeth unto God,
> It is sealed with His finger.

Finally, there is the attribute of loving-kindness which also belongs to Amen-em-ope's conception of

---

[1] Griffith renders this line : ' Nor labour to seek strife (*sic*), possibly in reference to God ; the meaning then would be that a man must not seek to justify himself in the sight of God.

God. ' Commit thyself into the arms of God ' (Griffith renders : ' Sit thee down at the hands of God ') is one of his utterances ; it occurs three times ; twice it refers to placing one's cause in God's hands (xxi., xxii.), and in the other passage, which will come before us again, it is in reference to a man's behaviour to his enemy. But in each case the words are obviously prompted by the writer's conviction of God's loving-kindness. It has already been pointed out that Amen-em-ope tended to be monotheistic, but that he was not a monotheist. Whether he regarded the sun as a symbol of Re, the sun-god, or of the All-Ruler, cannot be said with certainty ; but his thought of divine loving-kindness is certainly illustrated by the following passage :

Pray to the sun (Aten) when it riseth,
And say—' Give me prosperity and health ' ;
Then will he give thee what thou needest for thy life,
And thou wilt be free from fear. (VII. x. 12–15.)

No words, however, could witness more fully to the writer's living trust in the divine loving-kindness than those in which he speaks of the joy of the man who is safe with God in the life hereafter :

How happy is he who hath reached the West [1]
And is safe in the hand of God. (XXV. xxiv. 19, 20.)

It will therefore be seen that Amen-em-ope's conception of God was an exalted one ; a distinct tendency towards a belief in one God, and at any rate an explicit recognition of an All-Ruler ; one Who alone is perfect ; the Creator of man, in Whose hands are life and death, Whose will is supreme, and in Whom the knowledge of the future lies. A God Whose outstanding attribute is righteousness, which He imparts to man ; in Whose

[1] The West land, or the Mountain of the West, was the abode of the dead.

all-seeing eye sin is an abomination ; but Who rejoices in the well-doing of men. A God Who has love for men, and Whose love can be relied upon both in this life and in the world to come.

The significance of this conception of God, as already pointed out, is enhanced when one compares it with the religious standpoint of the other Egyptian Wisdom books which are extant. This is not the place to make a detailed comparison [1] ; it is sufficient to say that the ' Teaching of Amen-em-ope ' stands alone, and is quite unique.

III. *Amen-em-ope's Teaching on the Duty of Man to his Fellow-creatures*

This subject is, in its way, as remarkable and as unique in the Egyptian Wisdom literature as the one just dealt with ; it is, therefore, also worth some little detailed consideration.

A good deal that has been said in the previous section applies here too, for the virtues and vices there mentioned as being either well-pleasing or abhorrent to God are shown forth in the behaviour of man towards his fellow-creatures. There must, therefore, be a little repetition here and there of some of the passages referred to, but as it will be in a different connexion this will not matter.

It is only right and fitting that a man should place a high value on the good opinion of others. In his Prologue Amen-em-ope mentions that one of the objects of his writing is that by following its guidance the praise of a man may be in the mouth of his fellows.

The means to this are manifold ; attention may first be drawn to the writer's general admonition :

[1] For the other Egyptian Wisdom writings see the translations in Erman's *Die Literatur der Aegypter*, pp. 86 ff., 294 ff. (1923).

See to it that thou be respected of men,
Then wilt thou be greeted by all.[1]   (VIII. x. 17, 18.)

Straightforwardness and frankness in speech are needed
for this :

Sever not thy heart from thy tongue,
Then will all be well with thee ;
Then wilt thou be held in esteem among the multitude,
And safe in the hand of God.   (X. xiii. 17–xiv. 1.)

Griffith renders this :

Sever not thy heart from thy tongue,
That all thy ways may be successful.
Be thou resolute before other people,
For one is safe at the hand of God.

And again :

Keep thy tongue from malicious speech,
So wilt thou make thyself loved of the people.
(VIII. x. 21–xi. 1.)

A fine piece of advice is given in this connexion, showing
by what a genuine sense of consideration for others
the heart of this Egyptian sage was animated :

When thou hearest good or bad (of people),
Put it aside as though thou hadst not heard it ;
Place the good upon thy tongue
But let the evil be hidden within thee.'[2]
(VIII. xi. 8–11.)

Griffith renders :

If thou hearest (to judge ?) a thing that may be either good
or bad,
Do this outside, (where) it is not heard ;
Put a good report upon thy tongue,
While the ill is hidden in thy belly.

[1] Griffith renders :

' Set thy goodness in the bowels of men
That everyone salute thee '

(i.e. ' accustom men to have a good opinion of thee planted in their
inmost soul ').
[2] Lit. ' in thy belly.'

The first line must mean, ' If thou hearest something which in thy judgment may be either good or bad.' That is admirable (cp. Ecclus. xix. 7, 8). A similar spirit is evinced in a passage in which the writer gives counsel regarding the attitude a man should take up towards one of a quarrelsome disposition ; there is some uncertainty about the meaning of one or two words, judging from the different ways in which they are rendered by experts ; but the general sense of the passage is perfectly clear :

> Do not irritate [1] a quarrelsome neighbour,
> And cause him not to utter the feelings of his heart.
> Haste not to enter his presence
> When thou seest not his purpose ; [2]
> First make sure of the purport of his words,
> And then be calm, and thus gain thine end.
> Leave him in peace, and let him say all he has to ; [3]
> Learn to be still,[4] and thou wilt gain him.[5]
> Take hold of his feet,[6] and do him no harm :
> Reverence him, and respect his feelings.[7]
>
> (XXII. xxii. 20–xxiii. 7.)

The inculcation of such self-control, consideration, and courteous behaviour towards a bad-tempered man is very striking ; one is irresistibly reminded of Prov. xv. 1 :

> A soft answer turneth away wrath,
> But a grievous word stirreth up anger ;

[1] The context seems to justify this word. Ranke renders : ' Do not listen to all that a quarrelsome neighbour has to say.' Lange translates : ' Do not challenge . . .' Griffith : ' Plot (?) not against thine opponent in debate,' but the meaning is uncertain.

[2] Presumably uncertainty as to the frame of mind he is in is meant.

[3] Griffith : ' Leave it to him that he may empty his inmost soul.'

[4] ' Learn to sleep.'

[5] Lit. ' he will be found,' which Lange takes to mean that he will disclose himself and become known in his true character.

[6] Lange says that this expression is not found elsewhere, and must have a similar meaning to ' kissing the feet,' *i.e.* showing honour to him.

[7] Lit. ' neglect him not ' (so Griffith), which Erman explains : ' by respectful behaviour thou wilt make him sympathetic.'

though it will be allowed that Amen-em-ope even surpasses this in his refinement of feeling. But a more striking thought-parallel is contained in Prov. xv. 18 :

> A wrathful man stirreth up contention,
> But he that is slow to anger appeaseth strife.

Cp. also Ben-Sira, Ecclus. xxviii. 8–12.

An admonition not to irritate a hot-tempered man with spiteful words occurs also in III. v. 10–14. Consideration for others prompts the prohibition not to tread in another's furrow (VI. viii. 15, 16). Courteous behaviour and respect towards others is enjoined in other passages ; thus in II. iv. 6, 7 it is said :

> Stretch not out thine hand to touch an old man,
> And be not the first to speak to thine elder.[1]

(See also XXVII. xxv. 17–xxvi. 1.)

A young man must show proper respect to his elders by waiting to receive recognition before claiming acquaintance, and he must hold his tongue until addressed by his betters. As Amen-em-ope pointedly remarks elsewhere :

> A man will not become poor by speaking courteously.
> (XXVI. xxv. 12.)

Again, in XXVI. xxv. 8–9 it is said that respect must be shown to an old man by others in the same way in which this is done by his own children. To one's superiors also due honour must be shown :

> Take heed that thou answer not thy superior,
> And guard thyself from insulting him.
> (IX. xi. 15, 16.)

Doing to others as you would wish to be done by is illustrated by Amen-em-ope in XXIX. xxvi. 16, 17 :

Suffer not a man to be left behind when crossing the stream,
While thou hast room and to spare in the ferry.

---

[1] Griffith : ' Nor snatch (?) at the word of the aged.'

He has also in mind what is due to those who are in misfortune, or who are unable to help themselves ; thus, a judge is admonished not to be the cause of ruining a man in a court of justice (XX.). Concerning the poor, the tax-gatherer is bidden to be merciful to a poor man (XIII.) ; and in II. iv. 4, 5 it is said :

> Beware of robbing the poor,
> And of oppressing the weak.[1]

And in regard to the man of small means he says :

> Covet not the goods of the small man,[2]
> And hunger not after his bread.   (XI. xiv. 5, 6.)

His thought is also for those suffering from bodily infirmities, and for those mentally deficient :

Laugh not at a blind man, and mock not at a dwarf,
And harm not him who is a cripple.[3]
Mock not at the man who is in the hand of God,[4]
And be not wrath (?) with him when he hath transgressed.[5]
(XXV. xxiv. 9–12.)

He utters a warning, too, against encroaching on a widow's land (VI. vii. 15).

But the most striking things which Amen-em-ope says about the duty of man to man are those which concern the evil-doer and a personal enemy. In speaking of him who has done wickedly. and whose sin has brought him to ruin, Amen-em-ope thus appeals to others :

[1] Griffith : ' Of being valorous against the man of broken arm.' Ranke : ' nor make thyself strong against ' ; Erman similarly.

[2] Griffith : ' a dependent.'

[3] ' Nor mar the design of a lame (?) man ' (Griffith) ; it probably means, he says, that one must not ' play some practical joke to hinder his movements.'

[4] A man who is ' in the hand of God ' means, according to Lange and Ranke, one who is mentally deficient ; this is also what is meant by the phrase among the Egyptians at the present day.

[5] So Griffith ; Lange : ' when he lacketh (understanding).'

Raise him up, give him thy hand,
Lay him in the arms of God ;
Fill him with bread in thy home,[1]
That he be sated, and come to himself.[2]

(II. v. 3-6.)

In the same chapter a prayer is addressed to the Moon-god (probably regarded as a symbol of the All-Ruler) on his behalf :

Thou moon, who hast certified his sin (Griffith : ' bring
    forward his crime '),
Guide the wicked one that he come over to us,
To us, who have not done as he hath done.[3]

(II. iv. 19-v. 2.)

As to a man's attitude to his enemy Amen-em-ope writes thus :

Pause before an intruder (or, enemy),
And give way unto him that attacketh.[4]   (III. v. 12.)

A still more striking example is that contained in XXI. xxii. 1-4 ; Lange renders :

Say not, ' Find me a powerful ruler,
I will take vengeance on a man in thy city,'
Say not, ' Find me . . .
Now I shall be able to avenge me on mine enemy ' (lit. ' the
    hated one ').

In these words Amen-em-ope bids a man refrain from injuring his enemy even when, through the protection of one in authority, the opportunity may be offered of

---

[1] Griffith also supports this rendering now (in a private communication).

[2] ' And come to himself,' or the knowledge of himself, may or may not represent the original. Lange confesses that his rendering of the word is only a guess. Ranke translates it ' And twinkle (*i.e.* with his eyes) again happily ' ; but he queries it.

[3] Griffith divides differently and renders the last two lines :

' Steer, that we may carry the bad man over,
    For we will not do as he (hath done).'

[4] This is Griffith's rendering.

taking vengeance without fear of reprisals. Griffith renders the passage in this way :

Say not, ' Find me a strong chief,
For a man in thy city hath injured me ' ;
Say not, ' Find me a redeemer,
For a man who hateth me (or, whom I hate) hath injured me.'

He believes that the imperative, 'Find me . . .,' not the perfect, must be used here. The word which he translates ' redeemer' is, according to Lange, a hitherto unknown word ; but Griffith connects it with a well-known root and the context demands a word like this ; presumably it is used, much as in Hebrew, in the sense of ' vindicator,' or ' avenger.' The precept which the Egyptian sage thus puts forth witnesses to a high ethical ideal, above all for the times in which it was written, when vengeance on an enemy was looked upon not only as a natural proceeding, but almost as a duty.

It will thus be seen that Amen-em-ope's religious standpoint regarding the two cardinal aspects of religion, the conception of God, and duty to one's fellow-creatures, is of a high order. His thoughts and teaching about God, and his precepts on men's behaviour to one another, are confessedly unique in Egyptian Wisdom literature. One may, indeed, go farther, and assert without fear of contradiction that the like is not to be found elsewhere in the ancient literature of pre-Christian times, with the one exception of the Hebrew Scriptures.[1]

---

[1] It is not forgotten that there are a number of passages both in Egyptian and Babylonian hymns which are very beautiful, and which breathe a religious spirit comparable to many passages in the Psalms ; but these are isolated passages. What strikes one about Amen-em-ope's book is that the whole of it is imbued with the two-fold religious aspect of the thought of the Deity and duty to one's fellow-men. The motive of the latter is the God-ward sense ; that is what is especially noteworthy.

This fact is of paramount interest and importance. And the question arises as to whether there is any relationship between Amen-em-ope's writing and the Old Testament; and if so, what the nature of that relationship is. But before we can be in a position to reach any conclusions on that question it is necessary to take a brief glance at those historical periods during which the intercourse between Egypt and Palestine was such as to afford possibilities for mutual mental and literary influence. It is also necessary to compare together some passages of the book of Amen-em-ope with some of those in the Old Testament books.

His work belongs to Wisdom literature; we shall, therefore, naturally start by comparing it with the foremost Wisdom book in the Old Testament, the Book of Proverbs; and some astonishing parallels, possibly something more than mere parallels, will be found to exist. We shall then turn to the more directly religious elements in the Egyptian writing and compare them with some of the teaching contained in the Book of Deuteronomy; here, too, some interesting affinities will be observed; and finally, we shall make some miscellaneous comparisons between Amen-em-ope and certain passages from other Old Testament books, especially from the Psalms, which, it is hoped, may also help us in reaching some conclusions regarding the nature of the relationship between the ' Teaching of Amen-em-ope ' and the Hebrew Scriptures.

CHAPTER III

ISRAEL AND EGYPT

THE periods during which there was contact between the people of Israel and Egypt prior to about 1000 B.C. do not, for our present purpose, come into consideration. The Israelites before this time, and indeed for at least a couple of centuries later, were not sufficiently advanced in the religious domain to influence others in this direction. Some traces of Egyptian influence on Hebrew religion may possibly be discerned, *e.g.* the worship of the Golden Calf, though this is by no means certain ; but in all probability the effect of such influence would have been only transient, and in any case would not have been of such a nature as to concern us in the present connexion. As to literature, it can hardly be said that such a thing existed among the Israelites at this time.

The first contact between Israel and Egypt which concerns us here was in the reign of Solomon. He came to the throne about the year 970 B.C. In 1 Kings iii. 1 it is recorded : ' And Solomon made affinity with Pharaoh king of Egypt, and took Pharaoh's daughter, and brought her into the city of David. . . .' (cp. vii. 8) ; and ix. 16 tells of Pharaoh having given Gezer ' for a portion unto his daughter, Solomon's wife.' [1] The two kingdoms were, according to 1 Kings iv. 21, contiguous at this time, as Solomon's

---

[1] The Pharaoh in question was perhaps Siamon (*circa* 970–950 B.C.) according to Hall, *The Cambridge Ancient History*, iii. p. 257 (1925).

rule is said to have extended to 'the border of Egypt.'
The boast that Solomon's wisdom excelled ' all the
wisdom of Egypt' (1 Kings iv. 30) is due to the post-
exilic redactor; the note is interesting in another
connexion (see p. 99), but does not concern us here.[1]
The passage which deals with the purchase of horses
from Egypt by Solomon (1 Kings x. 28, 29; cp.
Deut. xvii. 16), where the text is corrupt, is too uncertain to build much on.

Contact between Egypt and Palestine is next
indicated in 1 Kings xi. 40. Here it is said that
Jeroboam, in order to escape Solomon's wrath, 'fled
into Egypt, unto Shishak king of Egypt, and was in
Egypt until the death of Solomon.' The Pharaoh
here mentioned is Sheshonk I, the first king of XXII
(Libyan) dynasty (945 B.C.). The friendliness shown
to Jeroboam was reversed later. In the reign of
Rehoboam Shishak attacked Jerusalem, and ' took
away the treasures of the house of Jahweh, and the
treasures of the king's house' (1 Kings xiv. 25, 26;
cp. 2 Chron. xii. 2, 9, 11). This was the first Egyptian
invasion of Palestine for several centuries; an account
of the campaign, which took place about 930 B.C.,
occurs on an inscription on the ' Bubastite Gate' of
the great temple at Karnak; according to this account
the northern as well as the southern kingdom was
invaded; but no reason is given either in the Old
Testament or in the inscription for the change of
friendly relations between Shishak and Jeroboam.
Probably there was no reason; the Egyptian king
was not likely to let anything of such a nature stand
in the way of his designs.

Some twenty-five years after this another Egyptian
invasion of Judah took place. This is not recorded
in the Book of Kings; but in 2 Chron. xiv. 9 ff. it is
told how Zerah the Ethiopian came to Mareshah with

[1] See further Stade, *Geschichte des Volkes Israel*, i. pp. 309 f. (1886).

a great army, but was defeated by Asa (see also
2 Chron. xvi. 8). This was about the year 895 B.C.
It is a matter of uncertainty as to which Pharaoh is
represented by the name Zerah. Hall has little doubt
that it was Osorkhon who was meant ; but S. A. Cook
thinks that ' the name Zerah can hardly be identified
with that of Osorkhon I.' [1] There are, however, considerable difficulties surrounding the record of this
invasion.[2]

We hear now of no further attacks on either of the
Palestinian kingdoms by Egypt ; the country ' sank
into an apathetic sloth, which, however, was wealthy
and comfortable enough, to judge from this Osorkhon's
list of magnificent gifts which he bestowed on the gods,
chronicled by him in the temple of Bubastis.' [3]

Incidentally, mention may be made of the fact that
Ahab of Israel and the Musri were among the con-
federates who were defeated by the Assyrians at the
battle of Karkar, 853 B.C.[4] Some hold that by the
Musri the Egyptians are meant ; this is, however,
improbable ; apart from other reasons, the contingent
sent, 1000 infantry, would be very insignificant for
a country like Egypt. It is more likely that the
reference is to the people of this name who lived in
or beyond the Taurus range.[5]

Otherwise no further intercourse is recorded until
just before the downfall of the northern kingdom.
Hoshea, hoping with the help of Egypt to throw off
the yoke of his Assyrian overlord, ' sent messengers
to So, king of Egypt, and offered no present to the
king of Assyria, as he had done year by year '
(2 Kings xvii. 4). Nothing is said about the response,
if there was one, from Egypt. We are only told that

---

[1] *Camb. Anc. Hist.*, iii. pp. 261, 360.
[2] See Peet, *Egypt and the Old Testament*, pp. 164 ff. (1922).
[3] Hall, *op. cit.*, iii. p. 261.
[4] The Black Obelisk of Shalmaneser II in the British Museum.
[5] *Camb. Anc. Hist.*, iii. p. 140.

' the king of Assyria shut him up, and bound him in prison.' [1]

The trust placed in Egypt for help against the power of Assyria was not confined to the northern kingdom. It is clear from the Old Testament that in the time of Hezekiah (*circa* 720–691 B.C.) there was a strong Egyptian party in Judah, headed by the king himself, a party which was in close touch with Egypt, to whom they looked for help against the Assyrian menace which was approaching. The most vehement opposer of the Egyptian alliance fostered by Hezekiah was the prophet Isaiah. In one of his prophecies he says : ' Woe to the rebellious children, saith Jahweh, that take counsel, but not of me . . . that walk to go down into Egypt, and have not asked at my mouth ; to take refuge in the refuge of Pharaoh, and to trust in the shadow of Egypt. Therefore shall the refuge of Pharaoh be your shame, and the trust in the shadow of Egypt your confusion . . .' (Isa. xxx. 1–5). And again : ' Woe unto them that go down to Egypt for help, and gaze (so the Septuagint) on horses, and trust in chariots because they are many, and in horsemen because they are very strong. . . . For the Egyptians are men, and not God ; and their horses are flesh, and not spirit ; and when Jahweh shall stretch out his hand, he that helpeth shall stumble, and he that is holpen shall fall, and they all shall fail together' (Isa. xxxi. 1–3).

These passages give us a good insight into the close relationship between Judah and Egypt at this time. It is in the light of them that we must read 2 Kings xviii. 19 ff. : ' . . . Now on whom dost thou trust, that thou hast rebelled against me ? Now, behold, thou trustest upon the staff of this bruised reed, even

---

[1] For discussions on ' So, king of Egypt,' see *Camb. Anc. Hist.*, iii. pp. 58, 275 f., Peet, *op. cit.*, pp. 171 ff.   He was probably tartan of Piankhi.   See a recent article by H. M. Wiener in *Ancient Egypt* for June 1926, pp. 51–53.

upon Egypt, whereon if a man lean, it will go into his hand and pierce it ; so is Pharaoh king of Egypt unto all that trust on him.' These are the words spoken to Hezekiah by the Rabshakeh in the name of the Assyrian king, Sennacherib, after the defeat of the allies at the battle of Eltekeh, near Ekron (700 or 701 B.C.) ; see further, 2 Kings xviii. 13–16.[1]

The mention of Tirhakah, king of Ethiopia, in connexion with Hezekiah (2 Kings xix. 9) offers a further indication of the relationship between Judah and Egypt ; but it raises a perplexing problem ; with this, however, it is unnecessary to deal here.[2]

The efforts made by Egypt to stem the tide of Assyrian conquest were in vain. We need not follow out the steps of the country's downfall ; suffice it to say that with the fall of Thebes in 663 B.C., under Ashur-bani-pal Assyrian supremacy over Egypt was complete.

This condition of things did not, however, last long. Ashur-bani-pal appointed Psammetichus ruler of Egypt under his overlordship, after the fall of Thebes. Psammetichus, the founder of the XXVI dynasty, was a man of outstanding energy and ability. He seized the first opportunity of regaining the independence of his country, when, owing to Ashur-bani-pal being busy fighting the Elamites and quelling revolts in Babylonia, Egypt was likely to be left in peace. At the same time, as Hall points out, his attitude towards Ashur-bani-pal was friendly. 'The policy which had insured to Psammetichus the kingship, and had preserved Egypt from further outrage, was one of subservience, more or less, to Assyria. But as time went on his position in regard to Ashur-bani-pal must have altered sensibly from one of hardly disguised subject-alliance to one of

---

[1] What is here said is confirmed by the account of Sennacherib's victory recorded on the Taylor Cylinder in the British Museum.
[2] See *Camb. Anc. Hist.*, iii. pp. 74, 278 f. ; Peet, *op. cit.*, pp. 175 ff.

a frank alliance of equals, in which, however, the main obligation was on the side of Egypt. The Pharaoh owed his position to Assyria, and he did not forget it. Till the end of his life he was the faithful ally of Assyria, and we have the extremely significant fact that when Asia had been shaken and her political face altered by the Scythian invasion Psammetichus appears as actively intervening in the interests of Assyria.' [1]

Continuing this policy, Necho, the son of Psamme-tichus, sent troops to help an Assyrian army which sought to regain Harran [2]; for in spite of the fall of Nineveh in 612 B.C. Assyria had still some life left in her. The attempt was unsuccessful; but in 608 B.C. Necho himself led his army northwards. It is on this occasion that we once more hear of contact between Palestine and Egypt. In 2 Kings xxiii. 29, 30, we read: ' In his (i.e. Josiah's) days Pharaoh-necho king of Egypt went up against the king of Assyria to the river Euphrates; and king Josiah went against him; and he slew him at Megiddo, when he had seen him. And his servants carried him in a chariot dead from Megiddo, and brought him to Jerusalem, and buried him in his own sepulchre.' This account represents Necho as going to fight against Assyria; but the fuller account in 2 Chron. xxxv. 20 ff. says that ' Necho king of Egypt came up to fight against Carchemish by Euphrates; and Josiah went out against him. But he sent ambassadors to him, saying, What have I to do with thee, thou king of Judah? I come not against thee this day, but against the house wherewith I have war. . . . Nevertheless Josiah would not turn his face from him, but disguised himself that he might fight with him, and hearkened not unto the words of Necho . . .

---

[1] *Camb. Anc. Hist.*, iii. pp. 294 f.

[2] This had been the seat of the Assyrian government until it was captured by the Scythians in 610 B.C.

and he died, and was buried in the sepulchre of his fathers.' The account given by Josephus agrees in the main with this ; he says that Necho's object was ' to fight with the Medes and Babylonians who had overthrown the dominion of the Assyrians, for he had a desire to reign over Asia.' Josephus also makes it clear that Necho had no wish to fight with Josiah.[1] These two more circumstantial accounts, though later, seem on the whole to have preserved a better version of the incident.[2]

After this Necho interfered drastically in the affairs of Judah. He first deposed Josiah's successor, Jehoahaz, and ' put him in bands at Riblah in the land of Hamath, that he might not reign in Jerusalem,' and afterwards took him to Egypt, where he died (see Ezek. xix. 3, 4). He then laid the land under tribute, and set up another son of Josiah, Eliakim, as king, changing his name to Jehoiakim. Of this latter it is said that he ' gave the silver and gold to Pharaoh ; but he taxed the land to give the money according to the commandment of Pharaoh ' (2 Kings xxiii. 32 ff.). The custom of a change of name on the accession to the throne was common. It was perhaps a concession to national feeling on the part of Necho in changing the new king's name from Eliakim to Jehoiakim ; at any rate it points to the interest that the Egyptian king took in the reform which was being attempted in Judah in the interests of a purer Jahweh worship. The fact is an indication that a knowledge of Jewish religious affairs existed in Egypt.

The position which Egypt had gained did not last long. At the battle of Carchemish (605 B.C.) Necho was defeated by Nebuchadrezzar, and, as the Old Testament says, ' the king of Egypt came not again any more out of his land ; for the king of Babylon

---

[1] *Antiq.*, X. v. 1.
[2] See further *Camb. Anc. Hist.*, iii. p. 395.

had taken, from the brook of Egypt unto the river Euphrates, all that pertained to the king of Egypt ' (2 Kings xxiii. 7 ; cp. Jer. xlvi.).

Judah had now as its suzerain Babylon in place of Egypt ; and for three years Jehoiakim submitted to Nebuchadrezzar (2 Kings xxiv. 1). But, as in former times, so now there was a strong Egyptian party in Judah ; and Jehoiakim rebelled against his suzerain, trusting, as we must suppose, that Necho would support him. But Necho did nothing for his vassal king, and Jehoiakim came to a miserable end. In Jer. xxii. 19 it is said, in reference to him, ' he shall be buried with the burial of an ass, drawn and cast forth beyond the gates of Jerusalem.' His son, Jehoiachin, was barely seated on the throne when Nebuchadrezzar appeared before the gates of Jerusalem. Jehoiachin submitted to him, but was carried captive, together with the chief men of the land, to Babylon (2 Kings xxiv. 13-16). In his place Nebuchadrezzar set Mattaniah, another son of Josiah, on the throne, changing his name to Zedekiah (2 Kings xxiv. 17 ; Ezek. xvii. 12-14). For a short time he remained loyal ; but soon, with hopes again set on Egypt, he rebelled. Apries (Hophra) was now the Pharaoh, and he supported Zedekiah in his revolt against Babylon (cp. Ezek xvii. 15-17). What happened to the Egyptians is not clear (cp., however, Jer. xliv. 30) ; but Nebuchadrezzar was soon again before Jerusalem, which was taken after a short siege. Zedekiah attempted to escape, but he was captured and taken to Riblah, where the king of Babylon was. Here his sons were slain before his eyes ; he himself was blinded, bound in fetters, and carried away to Babylon (2 Kings xxv. 1-7) with the other exiles.

Gedaliah was appointed governor of Judah, and after seven months he was murdered by some of the ' seed royal ' of Judah. In fear of what the consequences of this act might be, ' all the people, both small and great,

arose and came to Egypt' (2 Kings xxv. 26), which
suggests that this revolt, too, was instigated by Egypt.
Jeremiah protested strongly against this flight into
Egypt, but was taken there with the rest by Johanan
and his followers. They settled down in Tahpanhes
(Jer. xliii. 1-7), or Daphnae, on the Eastern Delta.

According to Jer. xliv. 1 (cp. xlvi. 14), there were
Jewish settlements in the north of Egypt—Migdol,
Tahpanhes—Noph (Memphis) in central Egypt, and
Pathros in southern Egypt. This is a wide area
and these settlements must have existed before
Jeremiah's time. They point to considerable intercourse between Egypt and Palestine. During the reign
of Psammetichus, in the middle of the preceding
century, it is known that the settlement of foreigners
was encouraged both as traders and mercenaries[1];
these settlements, like that at Elephantiné, may have
originated then. It is also known that the Jews of
the Dispersion kept up intercourse with their brethren
in the homeland; an instance of this is given in the
Elephantiné papyri; they may well, therefore, have
formed one medium whereby Egyptian influences
penetrated into Palestine.

These then are, put very briefly, the chief indications
we have of intercourse between Israel and Egypt. As
they stand they do not seem to suggest that the
relationship between the two peoples was such as would
have been likely to further conditions under which
literary or religious influences would operate.

But these indications offer only one side of the
picture; and while they deal confessedly only with
historical facts, they offer glimpses here and there of

[1] Peet, *op. cit.*, p. 189; *Camb. Anc. Hist.*, iii. p. 294. Meyer, *Der
Papyrusfund von Elephantiné*, pp. 32 ff. (1912); there is also refer-
ence, though regarding a slightly later time, to Jews in Egypt in the
Letter of Aristeas, § 13, where it says that Psammetichus, king of
Egypt, used Jewish mercenaries in his campaign against Ethiopia.
It is Psammetichus II who is meant, 595-590 B.C.

relationships of a different character : such, for example, as the reference to the wisdom of Egypt (1 Kings iv. 30 ; Isa. xix. 11 ff.). Nor must the significance of what seems to have been a more or less permanent element in Jerusalem be overlooked, viz. the Egyptian party ; though politics was the main concern here, the constant dealings with Egypt necessarily involved a familiarity with things Egyptian generally ; and in this way, too, the possibility must be contemplated of Israelite religious thought having affected Egyptian visitors.

We shall refer again to the subject in the concluding chapter.

CHAPTER IV

THE 'TEACHING OF AMEN-EM-OPE' AND THE BOOK OF PROVERBS

I. *Some Contrasts between the Two Books*

THE relationship between these two Wisdom books is so evident, even to a superficial reader, that it has necessarily attracted more attention than any other question to which the discovery of the Egyptian book has given rise.

It is only necessary to run one's eye over one of the translations of Amen-em-ope's writing which have been published to see at once that it belongs to the same class of literature as the Book of Proverbs. The thoughts are often different between the two books; and the mode of expression in Amen-em-ope is, as one would naturally expect, in many cases very unlike anything we read in Proverbs; but there is no mistaking the fact that both books are representatives of Wisdom literature, using this term in its widest sense. At the same time, there are one or two points of contrast, not in themselves important, which are worth bearing in mind. These may be first briefly alluded to.

The Book of Proverbs contains, in the main, comparatively short and pithy sayings, whereas Amen-em-ope, as already mentioned, is fond of much longer periods; not that short and pregnant proverbs are wanting in the latter, as illustrations to be given presently will show; but the Egyptian sage clearly prefers to enlarge upon a thought lest the reader should not fully grasp its import. Sometimes Amen-em-ope seems to take some proverb as the text for a miniature discourse; at other times he drives home the point of such discourse by quoting a proverb in illustration.

As an example of the more extended form, the following from IX. xii. 1–xiii. 9, describing a bad-tempered, evil-spoken man, may be quoted. The meaning of some parts is uncertain.

Swift is speech, when the heart is hurt,
More than wind before water (?).[1]
He is ruined and he is built up by his tongue,[2]
Yet he speaks an ugly (?) speech ;[3]
He makes an answer worthy of a beating,
(For) its freight (?) is of ill ;[4]
He makes a voyage like all the world ;[5]
But he is laden with false words.
He acts the ferryman (?) of weaving (?) speech,[6]
He goes and comes with wrangling.
When he eats, when he drinks within,
His answer is (heard) without.
Verily the day of charging his crime
Is a misery for his children.
Would that Khnum[7] might bring in indeed, indeed (?),
The potter's wheel for the fiery-mouthed,

[1] ' *I.e.* like the gusts which precede rain ; or perhaps " wind of the coast-land " ' (Griffith).

[2] Others render ' He destroyeth and buildeth up with his tongue.'

[3] Or ' calumnious speech.' Lange : ' When he speaketh evil ' ; Erman says the reference is to slander.

[4] Lange : ' The result of which is evil.'

[5] So, too, Erman and Ranke ; but Lange renders : ' He arouseth strife among men.'

[6] So Erman and Ranke ; Lange : ' He is a disputant who layeth snares with words.' The word rendered ' weaving ' is used of catching with a net (Ranke).

[7] Khnum is the potter who forms men.

To mould and burn hearts (like vessels),[1]

(And reform his ways![2] { These two lines are supplied
He is like a . . .)[2] { from the context, and do not
{ belong to the MS.

He is like a wolf's whelp in the farmyard,
He turns one eye contrary to the other ;
He sets brethren to wrangling.
He goes before every breeze like clouds,
He diminishes the colour of the sun ; [3]
He bends (?) his tail like a young crocodile,[4]
He gathers himself together, crouched (?),[5]
His lips are sweet, his tongue cold,[6]
But flame burns in his belly.
Leap not to cleave to that (fellow),
Lest a terror carry thee away.[7]

This example, which is one of many, illustrates the
extended style of proverb-writing of which Amen-
em-ope makes use, and it is in striking contrast to the
Book of Proverbs taken as a whole, though, of course,
we do get, in Chap. xxx. and elsewhere, a similar
miniature essay form.

In one particular Amen-em-ope's doctrine of retribution differs from that of the Book of Proverbs ; for in
the former reference is made to what will happen in
the future life as a consequence of behaviour in this
life. But otherwise the doctrine of retribution in the
two books is in agreement ; the motives of human

[1] This line ' is obviously corrupt, and is paraphrased here '
(Griffith).
[2] Griffith says here : ' I cannot but follow Lange's brilliant recognition of the drift of these lines, including the assumed omission of
two lines which are necessary to the arrangement in couplets.'
[3] The thought is of a sandstorm the effect of which is to obscure
the light of the sun (Lange).
[4] This is what the crocodile does when about to strike with his
tail (Lange).
[5] Erman : ' mutilated ' or ' cut short ' ; Griffith says ' the idea
may be that he crouches preparing to spring.' That this must be
right is borne out by the parallel passage in Ps. x. 10.
[6] Or ' his tongue bitter ' (Griffith) ; see also Lange, op. cit., p. 69.
[7] This line occurs also in VI. viii. 10.

action are prompted by what it entails in the present life. Thus, for example, Amen-em-ope teaches that the object of doing what is right is that a man may live long, or that it will bring prosperity (I., V., VI., X.; cp. Prov. i. 33; iii. 1, 2; iv. 10; x. 2; etc.). Sometimes prudent action is commended because of the beneficial effect it will have on a man's children (III. v. 18, 19; cp. Prov. xiii. 22; xiv. 26). On the other hand, there is a warning against the dire results that evil action will have on one's children (IX. xii. 13, 14).

Incidentally it may be added that with one exception (XXVIII. xxvi. 9, 10), where behaviour to a widow is spoken of (the exact meaning of the passage is uncertain), Amen-em-ope has nothing, good or bad, to say about women; in Proverbs there are very few chapters in which a reference of one kind or another is not made to women. Arising out of this it is also worth noting that Amen-em-ope never speaks of evil intercourse with women, which is somewhat prominent in Proverbs (see ii. 16–19; v. 1–23; vi. 20–vii. 27; ix. 13–18, all in the first collection of the book (i.–ix.)); cp. also Ben-Sira, vi. 2–4; xxiii. 16–27; xxv. 2; xxvi. 9–12.

II. *External Similarity between the ' Teaching of Amen-em-ope ' and the Book of Proverbs*

A few illustrations may first be given from Amen-em-ope, which may or may not have any parallel in Proverbs, in order to set forth the similarity in *form* between the two books. These will all be of the short, pithy type of proverb.

Here are two from Amen-em-ope, Chap. VII. x. 6, 7:

> Rejoice not in wealth (acquired) by theft.
> Nor groan over poverty.

Again :

> The ship of the covetous is left in the mud,
> But the boat of the silent one saileth on.
>
> (VII. x. 10, 11.)

The metaphor of the ship is used in another connexion, where it is said :

> The tongue of a man is the rudder of a ship,
> But the Universal Lord is its pilot.
>
> (XVIII. xx. 5, 6.)

The first line is strongly reminiscent of James
iii. 4, 5 : ' Behold the ships also, though they are so
great, and are driven by rough winds, are yet turned
about by a very small rudder, whither the impulse of
the steersman willeth. So the tongue also is a little
member, and boasteth great things.' But it must be
allowed that Amen-em-ope puts the idea on a higher
plane by insisting that the human ship is really guided
by the divine Pilot.

A curiously expressed proverb is one contained in
XXIV. xxiv. 4, 5, which runs :

> The heart of man is the nose of God (or, of a god),
> Beware of neglecting it.

The phrase ' the nose of God ' recalls a somewhat
similar one in XV. xvii. 7, ' the beak of the Ibis ' (' The
finger of the scribe is the beak of the Ibis ') ; it was in
this bird that the god Thoth was believed to appear ;
he was the patron of scribes. Griffith says that the
phrase here can be rendered ' the beak of God,' referring
to Thoth (so Ranke), apparently meaning that a man's
conscience (heart) is, as it were, the organ by which
God discerns right and wrong, *i.e.* in a man. On the
other hand, Thoth is only mentioned in this book when
reference is made to what was especially under his
guardianship, scales and weights (XVI. xvii. 18–xviii. 5),
and the scribe and his art (XV. xvii. 7–12), while in

this passage it is only a question of a noble and his
dependent.   The preceding couplet to this one runs :

> Let not thy speech be carried abroad,
> Lest thine heart be bitter (?).[1]

(XXIV. xxiv. 2, 3.)

One might therefore paraphrase the whole thus: Repeat
not what thou hearest in the house of a noble, lest thou
rue it ; for thy fate depends upon the king who hands
out the breath of life ; do not forget this.

Another example showing general similarity in form
with Proverbs is the following :

Man is clay and straw, God is his builder,
He destroyeth and buildeth up daily ;
He maketh a thousand small, according to his will,
And he maketh a thousand to be in high place (lit. ' over-
    seers ').
When he is in his hour of life.   (XXV. xxiv. 13–18.)

Griffith is of opinion that a line has dropped out before
this last line.   This passage is one of several in which
' God ' is used without the article.   Referring to this,
Lange says : ' Amen-em-ope speaks of " God " and
" the God," just as the Mohammedan says Allah and
il-Allah, but there is no difference of meaning between
the two.' [2]   The same usage is found in both earlier
and later writers of this class of literature, according
to Wallis Budge, who does not think that when Amen-
em-ope speaks of ' God ' he is referring to Rê, Atēn,
or other gods mentioned by him.   If this were a
funerary text it would be different, for in these ' God '
is frequently used in reference to Osiris.[3]

Two more examples showing the close parallel of
type, so far as outward form is concerned, may be
given :

----

[1] Griffith's rendering.   [2] *Op. cit.*, p. 19.
[3] Op. cit., p. 147.

> Receive no gift from one who is powerful,
> And oppress not the poor for his benefit.[1]
>
>   (XX. xxi. 3, 4.)

' Gift ' here, as in the Old Testament usage in such connexions, must be equivalent to ' bribe.'

The other occurs likewise among admonitions to the judge, who is bidden not to bring a man into misfortune by a travesty of justice, and it is added :

> Be not influenced by fine clothes,
> And refuse not him that is in rags.[2]
>
>   (XX. xxi. 1, 2.)

This reminds one again of the Epistle of James ii. 2 ff., where, though in a different connexion, it is said : ' For if there come into your synagogue a man with a gold ring, in fine clothing, and there come in also a poor man in vile clothing ; and ye have regard to him that weareth the fine clothing, and say. . . .'

These few examples, then, illustrate the general similarity between Amen-em-ope and Proverbs in literary form.

III. *Parallelism in Thought, and some Verbal Identities*

A number of parallels have been gathered by Gressmann, and, later, by Simpson, in the article referred to. Most of these are sufficiently striking to suggest themselves to anyone familiar with both books. Some others are not so striking, at least not at first sight ; for these the present writer expresses his indebtedness

---

[1] Griffith renders : ' Nor repress the weak for him.'

[2] Griffith renders the couplet :

' Give not (all) thy attention to one that is clothed (?) in shining white,
And accept him in rags.'

to the two scholars mentioned ; a few additional ones which struck him when working on the subject are also given.

In the opening section of Proverbs the writer explains the objects for which proverbs should be studied ; in the same way Amen-em-ope, in the introduction to his book, tells of the benefits to be derived from his teaching. See Prov. i. 1–6, which concludes with :

That (a man) may understand a parable and a metaphor,[1]
The words of the wise and their riddles.

A similar thought seems to be in Amen-em-ope's mind when he says in I. iii. 9, 10 :

Give thine ears, hear (the words) that are said,
Give thine heart to interpret them.[2]

Immediately after these words he continues :

It is good to place them in thine heart,
But woe to him that refuseth [3] them.
Let them rest in the casket of thy belly,
That they may be a threshold (?) [4] in thine heart.

(I. iii. 11–14.)

This recalls Prov. vi. 20–22 :

Keep, my son, the commandment of thy father,
And reject not the instruction of thy mother ;
Bind them upon thine heart continually,
Tie them around thy neck (cp. i. 8, 9) ;

---

[1] The Hebrew word *melitzah* means a satirical saying, or the like (Hab. ii. 6), also an ' interpreter ' (Gen. xlii. 23) ; ' metaphor,' *i.e.* something which needs an interpretation, is a later meaning of the word, but is justified here on account of the ' dark sayings ' or ' riddles ' in the next clause.

[2] Griffith's rendering ; Ranke translates :
    ' Give me thy ears, and hear what I say,
      And direct thy heart to understand it ' (similarly Lange).

[3] Griffith : ' neglecteth.'

[4] So Griffith ; Lange ' lock,' Ranke ' key ' (?). The context in Proverbs would suggest ' guardian ' or the like (cp. vi. 22), if the original would permit of this here. As a threshold is something placed at an entrance, the idea of guardianship would seem to be a conceivable one.

When thou walkest it shall lead thee,
When thou liest down it shall keep guard over thee,
And when thou awakest, it shall talk with thee.

(Cp. iii. 21–24.)

Both passages contain the thoughts of giving heed
to wisdom, which must not be rejected, but kept in
the heart, so as to keep watch over a man. Four
parallel thoughts of this kind cannot be fortuitous:
they compel one to believe in a relationship between
the two books.

In the preceding verse in Proverbs, too, there is a
parallelism of thought; for in Prov. vi. 16–19, among
' seven things ' which are an abomination to Jahweh,
are:

An heart that deviseth wicked imaginations,
Feet that are swift in running to harm,
A false witness that uttereth lies,
And he who soweth discord among brethren.

In a passage from Amen-em-ope, quoted above
(IX. xii. 1–xiii. 9), the reference is to one who is ' laden
with false words,' who is guilty of ' calumnious speech,'
who ' layeth snares with words,' who ' setteth brethren
to wrangling,' and who ' goeth before every breeze
like clouds ' (= ' feet that are swift in running to
harm '). So that here again, although the passage
in Amen-em-ope contains many other thoughts as
well, it is difficult to resist the conviction that a
connexion exists between the two.

For Proverbs xi. 13a, see p. 58; Proverbs xi. 20,
see p. 55; Proverbs xii. 22, see p. 55; Proverbs xii. 23,
see p. 59. Further, in III. v. 13, 14 of the Egyptian
book we have:

Sleep a night before speaking.
The tempest ariseth as a flame in the straw.

There are at least two passages in Proverbs which lay

stress on the need of taking time before speaking lest evil consequences ensue :

Prov. xiii. 3. He that guardeth his mouth preserveth his life,
(But) he that openeth wide his lips—it is destruction to him.
xxi. 23. He that guardeth his mouth and his tongue, Guardeth himself from troubles.

The Hebrew uses different words for 'guard' in the two passages, *nôzēr* and *shômēr*, respectively. But both sages express in different ways the danger of a hasty tongue. The metaphor contained in Amen-em-ope occurs in Prov. xxvi. 21 :

Charcoal [1] to embers, and wood to fire,
And a contentious man to inflame strife.

So, too, in Ben-Sira :

Quarrel not with a loud-mouthed man,
And put not wood in fire.
(Ecclus. viii. 3 ; cp. xxviii. 8–12.) [2]

And James iii. 5–6 is also worth recalling : ' So the tongue is a little member and boasteth great things. Behold, how much wood is kindled by how small a fire. . . .'

It may be urged that an unbridled tongue is a thing so common among mankind that there is no occasion to suppose the influence of Amen-em-ope on Proverbs, or *vice versa*; if it were an isolated parallel the objection would be weighty, but the large number of them is what is so significant.

At any rate, here is a case in which some relationship

---

[1] So Toy. But by a slight emendation of the text Wildeboer would read ' bellows,' which is more appropriate.
[2] In the Psalms of Solomon, xii. 2, the tongue of a malicious man is compared with ' fire in a threshing-floor that burneth up the straw.'

between the two can hardly be denied ; in Amen-em-ope we read (VI. ix. 5–8) :

Better is poverty (or, a poor man) (being) in the hand of
  God [1]
Than wealth in the storehouse.
Better is bread with a happy heart
Than wealth with trouble.

A somewhat similar quatrain occurs in Chap. XIII.
xvi. 11–14 :

> Better is it to be praised as one loved of men [2]
> Than to have wealth in the storehouse.
> Better is bread when the heart is happy
> Than wealth with trouble.

These parallel thoughts are contained in the two
following passages in Proverbs :

> Better is a little with the fear of Jahweh
> Than great treasure and trouble therewith.
> Better is a portion of herbs where love is
>   (xv. 16, 17 ; cp. xvii. 1 and Eccles. iv. 6)
> Than a fatted ox and hatred therewith.
> Better is a little with righteousness
> Than great revenues with injustice.   (xvi. 8.)

Not far removed from this last is Amen-em-ope's
saying in Chap. VI. viii. 19, 20 :

> Better is one bushel given thee by God
> Than five thousand unjustly gained.

In Chap. XVIII. xix. 14–17 of Amen-em-ope's
book there is a passage which has caused much per-
plexity owing to the uncertainty of the meaning of
one word. The passage consists of four lines ; there
is no difficulty about the first two lines :

> God is in his perfection,
> Man is in his imperfection.

---

[1] The meaning of this phrase here, as the context shows, is different
from its use in the passage quoted above.
[2] Griffith renders: ' Better is praise and (?) love of men.'

The next couplet is rendered by Ranke :

> Scare away the words which men speak,
> Scare away that which God doeth.

This he explains (with a query, it is true) as meaning in effect : Do not worry about what men say, nor yet about what God does ; *i.e.* the words of men are not worth worrying about, and you cannot alter what God does, so it is no good worrying about that. Now it is certain that the last thing of which one could accuse Amen-em-ope is cynicism ; so that one can understand Ranke's query. The difficulty lies in the meaning of the word translated ' scare away ' (verscheuche) ; this Lange translates ' fade away,' and renders :

> The words which men speak fade away,
> And the deeds of God fade away.

But the second line here is in such direct contradiction with the first line of the first couplet that Lange assumed that a negative had fallen out in the last line, and that it should read : ' And the deeds of God fade not away.' But even so there is an incongruity in the contrast between the *words* of men and the *deeds* of God in such a connexion. Now Sethe has conclusively shown,[1] by a study of the use of the word translated ' scare away ' or ' fade away,' that its real meaning here is ' to be different ' ; and the second couplet must therefore be rendered :

> Different are the words which men speak,
> Different is that which God does.[2]

The Egyptians, as Sethe points out, are fond of using ' speaking ' for ' thinking,' so that the proverb

[1] *Der Mensch denkt* . . .
[2] Griffith renders :
> ' The words which men say are one thing
> The things which God doeth are another.'

means that what God does is different from what man thinks or plans ; it is, in fact, an ancient Egyptian form of the proverb : ' Man proposes, God disposes.' And the ancient Hebrew way of expressing it was :

> The heart of man deviseth his way,
> But Jahweh directeth his steps.
>   (Prov. xvi. 9 ; cp. xvi. 1 and xix. 21.)

So that we have here, in effect, a perfect parallel between Amen-em-ope and Proverbs.

It may be said here again, and the same may be held to apply in other instances to be cited, that the thought expressed is one which would naturally arise through human experience among different peoples, and that therefore such parallels are merely fortuitous. Under ordinary circumstances that objection would stand. But, as already remarked, we have to do here not only with isolated parallels ; there are a number of passages, as we shall see, in which the subject-matter is the same between the two books, and in which there is practical identity in both thought and word ; this precludes the idea of fortuitous agreement. That a definite relationship exists between the two does not admit of doubt ; the question is as to the nature of this relationship. Which influenced the other ? To that subject we shall come later ; for the present we are concerned with the *fact* of relationship.

In Chap. XVI. xvii. 18, 19, Amen-em-ope utters a prohibition to which there are at least three parallels in Proverbs :

> Move [1] not the scales, and falsify not the weights,
> And diminish not the parts of the corn-measure.

---

[1] The same word is used in VI. vii. 12 of removing a boundary stone. Griffith renders the couplet :
' Tamper not with the scales, nor falsify the *Kiti*-weights,
Nor diminish the fractions of the corn-measure.'

The three parallel passages in Proverbs are :

xvi. 11. Balance [1] and scales are Jahweh's,
His work are all the weights in the bag.
xx. 10. Divers weights and divers measures,
An abomination to Jahweh are they both.
xx. 23. An abomination to Jahweh are divers weights.
And deceptive balances are not good.

(Cp. also xi. 1.)

These, it is true, do not necessarily point to the influence of one or the other, for the practice condemned was common (cp. Am. viii. 5 ; Mic. vi. 11) ; but the parallel is worth drawing attention to.

Prov. xvii. 5. He that mocketh the poor reproacheth his Maker,
He that is glad at him that is perishing [2] shall not be unpunished.

With this compare Amen-em-ope XXV. xxiv. 9–12 :

Laugh not at a blind man, and mock not at a dwarf,
And harm not him who is a cripple.
Mock not at the man who is in the hand of God,
And be not wrath (?) with him when he hath transgressed. [3]

With the third line in Amen-em-ope may be compared Ben-Sira's couplet :

Mock not him who is in bitterness of spirit,
Remember there is One who exalteth and humbleth.

(Ecclus. vii. 11. Hebr.)

Prov. xviii. 6, 7. The lips of a fool lead to contention,
And his mouth calleth for stripes.
The mouth of a fool is his destruction,
And his lips are the snare of his soul.

---

[1] Omitting מֹשְׁפַט.

[2] Reading לְאֹבֵד (= Sept. τῷ ἀπολλυμένῳ) for לְאֵיד (' at calamity ').

[3] For the notes on this passage see above, p. 22.

Some lines from a passage from Amen-em-ope, quoted in another connexion (p. 37), are parallel in thought to this :

He is ruined and he is built up (or ' He destroyeth and
     buildeth up ') by his tongue,
Yet he speaketh an ugly (?) speech ;
He maketh an answer worthy of a beating,
(For) its freight (?) is of ill.[1]   (IX. xii. 3–6.)

It is evident that we have a real parallel in thought here.

Prov. xx. 9. Who can say, ' I have made my heart clean,
          I am pure from my sin ' ?

The sense of sin which these words witness to is no more than we should expect in a Biblical book ; but that, as we have already seen, it appears also in Amen-em-ope is a striking fact :

          Say not, ' I have no sin,'
          And be not at pains to (conceal it ?).[2]
                    (XVIII. xix. 18, 19.)

Proverbs xx. 10, see above, p. 49 ; Proverbs xx. 19, see below, p. 58 ; Proverbs xx. 22, see below, p. 56 ; Proverbs xxiii. 9, see below, p. 72.

Prov. xxiv. 11. Deliver those who are being taken away to
               death,
          And hide those who are tottering to their
               doom (lit. ' to slaughter ').

Scholars differ as to whom reference is made here ; a passage from Amen-em-ope may very likely be found to shed light on this.   In VIII. xi. 6, 7 it is said :

          Cry not ' crime ' at a man,
          Hide the manner of (a fugitive's) flight.

---

[1] For the notes on the passage see p. 37.
[2] See above, p. 16.

This is Griffith's rendering. It does not, perhaps, at first sight appear to be a parallel to the Proverbs passage; but in thought, at any rate, it will be seen that it is so. Pregnant as the first line is, its meaning is not doubtful when read in the light of the second, viz. one must not assume that because a man is a fugitive he is therefore a criminal; rather, do the merciful thing, and assist him in his flight by keeping it secret. The Egyptian sage, as the whole of his book shows, was far too upright a man to give such counsel in regard to a fugitive from justice; he is speaking of a fugitive from oppression. The compiler of Proverbs adapted this passage to the conditions that he saw in his own land, where cruelty and oppression were rife. Delivering from death, and not condemning a man as a criminal, are parallel thoughts.

In the second line in the Proverbs verse the Hebrew reads תִּמְשׁוֹךְ (lit. 'hold back'); it is a rare use of the word, and the Egyptian passage suggests the reading תַּמְשִׁיךְ ('hide'; cp. Ps. cxxxix. 12, and for the construction see Ps. cxxxix. 10). If, then, as seems justified, we have here a thought-parallel between the two books the verse in Proverbs must be understood as referring to the victims of oppression by the 'wicked' so often spoken of in the Psalms, and it can be interpreted in the light of such passages as Isa. lviii. 6, 7; Ps. lxxxii. 4. The objection that the expressions 'death' and 'slaughter' are too vigorous to be applied to the ordinary oppression of the poor by the rich (Toy), will hardly stand in view of such passages as Am. ii. 7, Hos. iv. 2, Ps. lxiv. 3-5 (Heb. 4-6), xciv. 3-6, a specially instructive passage, cix. 16, cxliii. 3, and others.

Proverbs xxiv. 29, see below, p. 56; Proverbs xxvii. 1, see below, p. 57; Proverbs xxvii. 14, see below, p. 54.

Again, in Chap. VI. viii. 15–18, Amen-em-ope says :

Tread not in the furrow of another ;
Better for thee it is to remain guiltless therefrom.[1]
Plough the fields, then wilt thou find what is needful,
And wilt obtain bread from thine own threshing-floor.

In turning to Prov. xxviii. 19 we read in the first line
of the verse a clear parallel to Amen-em-ope's first
line of the second couplet :

He that tilleth his land will be sated with bread ;

but the second line of this verse differs from Amen-em-
ope in being antithetical :

But he that followeth after vain men shall be sated with
want.[2]

It will not be denied that the balance between the
two Hebrew strophes leaves something to be desired.
It is true, ' sated with bread,' and ' sated with want '
form a perfect antithesis ; but ' he that tilleth his
land,' and ' he that followeth after vain men ' (or
things), is not so ; the proper antithesis to ' he that
tilleth his land ' would be ' he that suffereth his
land to lie fallow,' or the like. The parallel to
Prov. xxviii. 19 in Ben-Sira (xx. 28ª) offers a point
of some interest ; it is a line which is evidently not
quite at home in its place, for it can only be brought
into harmony with its context by means of a somewhat forced exegesis ; it runs :

He that tilleth his land raiseth high his heap.

This is a condensation of Amen-em-ope's third and
fourth lines ; and the reference to the ' heap ' (i.e. of
corn) is reminiscent of the ' threshing-floor.' This
suggests that Ben-Sira drew here from the Egyptian
book rather than from Proverbs, as in the cases

[1] This line is a little uncertain ; Griffith renders it : ' It is good for
thee to be sound in regard to them.'
[2] Prov. xii. 11 is almost identical with this verse.

mentioned on pp. 58, 59, 67 below; and probably other instances of the kind would be discovered by a detailed comparison between Ben-Sira's book and Amen-em-ope. That a copy of the latter may have come into Ben-Sira's hands in Palestine, just as was clearly the case with the compiler of Proverbs, is likely enough; we have the analogous instance of his own book in Egypt, as his grandson tells us in his prologue to the translation of the work: 'For having come into Egypt in the eight and thirtieth year of Euergetes the king, and having continued there some time, I found a copy [1] affording no small instruction. I thought it therefore most necessary for me to apply some diligence and travail to interpret this book. . . .'

With regard to the first couplet of the passage in Amen-em-ope, the first line, 'Tread not in the furrow of another' has a partial parallel in Prov. xxiii. 10[b]:

And enter not into the fields of the fatherless.

But this verse will come before us again in another connexion, p. 73.

IV. Chapters X and XXI of the 'Teaching of Amen-em-ope'

We have so far considered parallels which occur in quite different parts of the two books respectively. We shall now offer two examples of passages running consecutively in Amen-em-ope, but in which the parallels occur in different parts of the Book of Proverbs; and in the next section we shall take two examples of passages running consecutively in Proverbs; but in which most, though not all, of the parallels occur in different parts of Amen-em-ope.[2]

[1] On this difficult word (ἀφόμοιον) see Hart, *Ecclesiasticus, the Greek Text of Codex* 248, p. 264 (1909).
[2] For the object of this see the concluding chapter.

The two examples from Amen-em-ope are Chaps. X. and XXI. ; but they are not the only ones which could be used for the purpose, though they are the most striking.

Ch. X. xiii. 11. Salute not thy passionate (opponent),[1]
             forcing thyself,
         12. Nor grieve thine own heart (thereby) ;
         13. Say not to him, ' Hail to thee,' in falsehood,
         14. When there is terror in thy belly.[2]
Prov. xxvii. 14. He that saluteth [3] his neighbour with a loud
             voice,[4]
             It is equivalent to a curse to him.

This is a particularly interesting parallel because each of the two couplets in Amen-em-ope is a parallel to the Proverbs passage, and this latter can be explained in two ways, each being illustrated by the two couplets respectively ; thus, when a man salutes another ostentatiously, not really meaning what he says, forcing himself to do so, it is a curse to him ; *i.e.* he is ' grieving ' or damaging himself by doing so because he is guilty of a hypocritical act. This is equivalent to Amen-em-ope xiii. 11, 12. Another explanation is this : If a man salutes another ostentatiously, as a blind, because he fears him, and therefore meditates harm against him, it is ' a curse ' to him who is thus saluted. This is equivalent to Amen-em-ope xiii. 13, 14. In the Hebrew ' to him ' in the second line is ambiguous, as it can refer either to the saluter or to the saluted according as to how one interprets the first line. Now supposing our Egyptian sage had this passage before him (not, of course, in its present place,

---

[1] Ranke renders : ' . . . a passionate (man),' *i.e.* one with whom he has intercourse ; Lange ' . . . thy passionate (superior).'
[2] These lines are Griffith's rendering.
[3] Lit. ' blesseth ' ; but the Hebrew word can equally mean ' greet ' or ' salute,' see *e.g.* I Sam. xiii. 10 (R.V.) and elsewhere.
[4] The addition ' rising early in the morning ' is a gloss ; it breaks the rhythm.

but in some earlier source drawn upon by the compiler of Proverbs), and wished to make use of it for his own writing, and saw that it could be interpreted in two ways, would it not be a very natural proceeding if he adopted both interpretations and set them down in his book ? We are not saying that this is actually what Amen-em-ope did, but the possibility of this is worth considering.

But to continue :

> xiii. 15. Speak not to a man in falsehood,
> 16. The abomination of God ;
> 17. Sever not thy heart from thy tongue,
> 18. That all thy ways may be successful.[1]

There are two passages in Proverbs parallel with this :

> Prov. xii. 22. Lying lips are an abomination to Jahweh,
> But they who deal truly are his delight.
> xi. 20. They that are of crooked mind are an abomination to Jahweh,
> But such as are perfect in their way are his delight.

The chapter concludes with the following quatrain (Griffith's rendering) :

> xiii. 19. Be thou resolute (or, courageous) before other people,[2]
> xiv. 1. For one is safe in the hand of God.[2]
> 2. Hated of God is the falsifier of words,
> 3. His great abomination is the dissembler.

---

[1] These lines are Griffith's rendering. The last line is rendered by Erman, Ranke, and Lange with slight variations : ' Then it will happen that all thy affairs will be prosperous.'

[2] Erman, Ranke and Lange take these two lines as belonging to what precedes, and render, with slight variations :
' Then it will happen that thou wilt be esteemed by people,
And safe in the hand of God.'
But as there are three distinct quatrains it seems better to follow Griffith. On the other hand, these four lines read rather like two distinct couplets than one quatrain. The divisions are only conjectural, they are not in the original.

In view of the apparent uncertainty of the first line (see note), it is, perhaps, precarious to suggest a parallel; nevertheless, so far as the first two lines are concerned, the following is worth considering:

Prov. iii. 25. Be not afraid of sudden fear,
        Nor of the destruction of the wicked when it cometh;
    26. For Jahweh shall be thy confidence,
        And shall keep thy foot from snares.[1]
                  (Cp. verse 23.)

Two lines in Proverbs form the parallel to one in Amen-em-ope, in each case; but that does not affect the parallelism. 'Be courageous' among people is the same as 'be not afraid' of them, whether the reference is to words or acts; and in both there is the assertion of safety in God's hands.

Regarding the second couplet there are various passages in Proverbs which contain the same thought, but they can hardly be regarded as parallels (see, e.g., vi. 16, 17, 19; xxvi. 24).

We turn now to Chap. XXI. of Amen-em-ope; here, too, it will be seen that passage after passage has a parallel, more or less complete, in Proverbs. Some of the lines have come before us in other connexions, but a little repetition cannot well be avoided.

XXI. xxii. 1. Say not, 'Find me a strong chief,
      2. For a man in thy city hath injured me';
      3. Say not, 'Find me a redeemer,
      4. For a man who hateth me (or, whom I hate) hath injured me.'[2]

There are two parallels to this in Proverbs:

Prov. xx. 22. Say not, 'I will take vengeance for evil,'
        Trust in Jahweh, and he will save thee.
    xxiv. 29. Say not, 'As he did to me, so will I do to him,'
        I will repay a man according to his deed. (See also xvii. 13, and cp. xxv. 21, 22.)

---

[1] Lit. 'capture.'   [2] See further on this passage above, p. 23.

XXI. xxii. 5. Of a truth, thou knowest not the thoughts [1]
    of God,
    6. Thou canst not realise (?) the morrow ; [2]
    7. Place thyself in the arms [3] of God,
    8. Thy silence [4] will overthrow them.

This quatrain occurs again in XXI. xxiii. 8–11. With
the first couplet we may compare Prov. xxvii. 1 :

> Boast not thyself of to-morrow
> For thou knowest not what a day may bring forth.

Ben-Sira also says of the rich man :

> He knoweth not what the day may bring forth.
>   (Ecclus. xi. 19. Hebr.)

We are reminded once more of the Ep. of James iv.
13–16, especially verse 14 : ' Ye know not what shall
be on the morrow.'

So far as the second couplet is concerned no parallel
in Proverbs is forthcoming,[5] but with the first line
cp. Prov. xvi. 3 :

> Commit thy works unto Jahweh,
> And thy purposes shall succeed.

There follows in Amen-em-ope a couplet which reads
like some well-known proverb ; it is rendered by
Griffith :

xxii. 9. Verily a crocodile which is void of proclaiming,
    10. Inveterate is the dread of it.[6]

---

[1] Griffith : ' design.'
[2] So Griffith and Lange, but Erman and Ranke render : ' Thou
seest not the morrow.' With this couplet compare XVIII. xix. 12,
13 :
    ' Man knoweth not how the morrow will be,
    The events of the morrow are in the hands of God ' (Griffith).
[3] Griffith : ' Sit thee down at the hands of God.'
[4] Griffith : ' tranquillity.'
[5] See below, p. 83.
[6] The other translators are at a loss to render this line.

He comments on the expression ' void of proclaiming '
as ' a good example of far-fetched artificial expression,
standing for " soundless " or " dumb " ' ; and ' in-
veterate,' he says, means ' old.'   A parallel to this in
Proverbs, however, does not seem to be forthcoming.
Amen-em-ope continues :

xxii. 11. Empty not thine inner self [1] before all men,
    12. And harm not thine own influence (thereby) ;
    13. Let not thy words be spread abroad among others,
    14. And have thou nothing to do with the chatter-
      box.[2]

With the first couplet compare :

Prov. xxv. 9. Discuss thy business with thy neighbour
      (alone),
      And disclose not his secret to another.[3]
    10. Lest he that heareth it revile thee,
      And thine evil report depart not.

An even closer parallel is contained in Ben-Sira's
words :

    Never repeat what is told thee,
    Then no one will revile thee.
      (Ecclus, xix. 7,[4] and cp. xxvii. 16.)

With Amen-em-ope's second couplet (13, 14) compare :

Prov. xx. 19. He that goeth about as a tale-bearer revealeth
      secrets (= xi. 13[a]),
      And have thou nothing to do with him that
      openeth wide [5] his lips (= xiii. 3[b]).

---

[1] Lit. ' belly.'
[2] Griffith renders this line : ' Nor associate thyself with one who
lays bare his heart.'
[3] Reading סוֹדוֹ לְאַחֵר, so the Vulg. (Toy).
[4] See, on this passage, the present writer's *Ecclesiasticus*, p.
(Camb. Bible, 1912).
[5] For this meaning of *pathah* see Gen. ix. 27.

And, once more, Amen-em-ope says :

xxii. 15. He that (concealeth) his speech within himself [1]
16. Is better than he who uttereth it to (his) hurt.[2]
17. One doth not run [3] to achieve perfection.
18. One doth not throw to injure it.[4]

With the first couplet compare :

Prov. xii. 23. A prudent man concealeth knowledge.
But the heart of fools proclaimeth foolishness. (And cp. Ecclus. xix. 4.)

The second couplet is evidently a proverb, presumably illustrative of the preceding words. Lange
confesses he does not understand it ; nor do the other
translators throw light on it. It is, however, quite
possible that it may be explained by a passage in
Ben-Sira ; for in xi. 10 there are two couplets, which,
translated from the Hebrew, run :

My son, wherefore dost thou multiply thy business ?
Yea, he that hasteneth to increase (riches) shall not go
unpunished. (Cp. Prov. xiii. 11[a] = Sept. xxviii. 20[b].)
My son, if thou runnest thou wilt not attain,
And if thou haste thou wilt not find.

It is the second couplet which seems to represent
some form of the Egyptian proverb. The first line
in each is, in any case, essentially identical ; it is the
second line in the Egyptian text which the experts
find difficult. Griffith, in a private letter, says that
for ' throw ' one could perhaps translate ' produce ' ;
and for ' injure ' perhaps ' diminish.' So that possibly
the second line might be rendered :

One doth not produce in order to diminish.

The two couplets, then, in Amen-em-ope might be

---

[1] Lit. ' in his belly.'
[2] Griffith renders this couplet :
' Better is a man that (hides) his report within himself,
Than he who tells a thing to disadvantage.'
[3] Lange : ' haste.'   [4] Griffith : ' himself.'

paraphrased thus : Do not be in a hurry to blurt out your report in order to gain praise ; you will gain nothing by such precipitance, but rather lose in estimation. Then he illustrates this by the proverb, *i.e.* One does not run or haste to achieve perfection, nor does one produce (in this case the reference would be to the report) in order to injure or diminish (in this case reference would be to the messenger's reputation). So that we seem to have the adaptation of a well-known proverb to a particular case.[1] Ben-Sira apparently got hold of some form of this proverb which he adapted, and utilised to deprecate being in a hurry to amass wealth. The proverb is one which is widely applicable, like *Festina lente.*

It is certainly striking that there should be so much community of thought between these two chapters and the different passages in Proverbs ; and it is doubtful whether the illustrations given are exhaustive. They point without doubt to a relationship of some kind ; and the question is whether the writer of Proverbs in compiling his book utilised many of Amen-em-ope's sayings and adapted them to suit his Hebrew readers, or whether it was the other way round, and that Amen-em-ope made use of the Book of Proverbs, choosing what he thought suitable, and adapting this to his Egyptian readers, adding material of his own. We shall come to the consideration of this in our final chapter.

V. The ' Teaching of Amen-em-ope' and Prov. xxii. 17–xxiii. 14

All commentators are agreed that Prov. xxii. 17–xxiv. 22 forms a separate division, xxiv. 23–34 being

---

[1] Griffith, in a private letter, writes in reference to the above : ' Your suggestion as to the general meaning intended seems at least admissible.'

an appendix. It is, moreover, probable that this division consists of two collections : xxii. 17–xxiii. 14, and xxiii. 15–xxiv. 22 ; the latter is addressed to ' my son,' the familiar Jewish form of address found frequently in the first division of Proverbs (i. 1–ix. 18). This form of address does not occur in the other collections. Now this first collection of the two just mentioned (xxii. 17–xxiii. 14) is almost wholly paralleled in the ' Teaching of Amen-em-ope.' The order of the material is not the same in the two books, though some of the passages do follow consecutively in each. But when it is seen that practically the whole of this collection in Proverbs is found in the Egyptian book it is impossible to doubt that a relationship of some kind exists between the two.

Gressmann has gathered these parallels together in a convenient form in the article already referred to, and use has been made of his work. At the same time, the fact is that everyone familiar with the Book of Proverbs, when reading the translations of the ' Teaching of Amen-em-ope ' published by Erman, Ranke, Lange and Griffith, is bound to be struck by the obvious similarities between it and this collection (Prov. xxii. 17–xxiii. 14), quite apart from the many other parallels to a number of which attention has already been drawn.

We will now proceed to examine these parallels verse by verse, making a few emendations in the text of Proverbs where these seem called for and offering here and there some comments on the words of Amen-em-ope.

Prov. xxii. 17. Incline thine ear and hear my words,[1]
And apply thine heart to learn (them).[2]
A. I. iii. 9. Give thine ears, hear (the words) that are said,
10. Give thine heart to interpret them.[3]

[1] Following the Septuagint.   [2] Lit. ' to know,' reading לָדַעַת.
[3] See above, p. 43.

Here the two are practically identical ; no comment is needed.

Prov. xxii. 18. For it is a pleasant thing if thou keep them within thee (lit. ' in thy belly '),[1]
(And) if they be ready prepared [2] upon thy lips,
19. That thy trust may be in Jahweh, I have taught thee this day thy ways.[3]

A. I. iii. 11. It is good to place them in thine heart ;
12. —But woe to him that refuseth them,—
13. Let them rest in the casket of thy belly,
14. That they may be a threshold [4] in thine heart ;
15. That if a hurricane of words arise,[5]
16. They may be a check [6] upon thy tongue.

The general sense here is the same in both writings, though the marked differences must not be minimised ; the name of the God of Israel would naturally not occur in the book of an Egyptian priest, but would be inserted if an Israelite were utilising the Egyptian book. The last three lines in Amen-em-ope seem to be an expansion of ' thy ways ' in the Hebrew passage ; or else ' thy ways ' is a compression of Amen-em-ope.

It will be noticed that in the three verses of Proverbs so far quoted the parallel passages run consecutively in each book ; that is, of course, important from the point of view of the nature of the relationship between the two. In the next three parallel passages, however, the Egyptian parallels occur in three different places in the book.

[1] Cp. Prov. xviii. 8, xx. 27.
[2] Cp. Prov. xix. 29.
[3] Following the Septuagint, Gressmann reads אָרְחֹתֶיךָ (cp. iii. 6), which is preferable to the Massoretic text.
[4] See above, p. 43.
[5] Griffith : ' Verily (?) when there cometh a gale of speech.'
[6] Griffith : ' a mooring-post.'

Prov. xxii. 20. Have I not written for thee thirty . . .
            With counsels and knowledge !
A. XXX. xxvii. 7. Consider these thirty chapters ;
             8. They delight (and) they instruct ;
             9. They are the chief among all books,
            10. They make the unlearned wise.

In the Proverbs passage the Hebrew word here
rendered ' thirty ' is *shilshôm*, which means lit. ' three
days ago,' *i.e.* the day before yesterday, and might
conceivably be rendered ' formerly,' except that it
always occurs in combination with the word *temôl*
(used adverbially), and never alone.   If we suppose
that this word has fallen out of the text, and should
be supplied, the passage would refer to some former
writing.   But, as Toy rightly points out, ' this rendering is, in any case, improbable, for the reason that it
introduces a strange contrast between the instruction
now given to teach trust in Jahweh, and that formerly
given to impart the capacity of answering (verse 21).' [1]
The Hebrew margin gives *shalîshîm*, *i.e.* ' officers,'
which is meaningless here ; but some commentators
render this ' excellent things,' *i.e.* precepts, on quite
insufficient grounds.   The R.V., which has ' excellent
things ' in the text, writes in the margin : ' the word
is doubtful.'   Clearly the Hebrew text offers a great
difficulty here, and ' the embarrassment of the Greek
translators and expounders is shown by the variety
of readings in verses 19–20.' [2]
Now in the light of the parallel passage to this verse
in Amen-em-ope, Erman, by a very slight change in
the Hebrew word, read *shĕlôshim*, ' thirty ' ; and
Gressmann, adopting this, has shown that in this
division of Proverbs (xxii. 17–xxiv. 22, excluding the
introduction, xxii. 17–21) there are exactly thirty
proverbs, so that this number in the Hebrew text

---

[1] *Proverbs*, p. 423 (1914).   [2] Toy, *op. cit.*, p. 425.

referred originally to these thirty proverbs, the number
being based, as he contends, on the ' thirty chapters '
(lit. ' houses ') contained in the ' Teaching of Amen-
em-ope.' That the parallel passages occur almost
wholly in the first collection (xxii. 17–xxiii. 14) of the
division would not, in any case, invalidate Gressmann's
contention, as the division forms one whole ; but,
as a matter of fact, there is one parallel in the later
portion (xxiv. 11). We may take it, then, that
shĕlôshim, ' thirty,' is what we should read in the
Hebrew text, and it may conceivably have originally
added a noun, as in 1 Kings iv. 32 (v. 12 in Hebr.),
' thirty proverbs,' or the like, though this is not
necessary ; for, as Gressmann says, where·indications
of measures, weights, and time are concerned, the
noun is usually omitted,[1] since there is no doubt as
to what is referred to.

The parallelism in these passages centres in the
' thirty.' Amen-em-ope is again more verbose, indeed,
he continues for several lines, but it is unnecessary
to quote them. They simply elaborate the ' counsels
and knowledge ' of Proverbs. Or is it that Proverbs
compresses Amen-em-ope ? That is an interesting
point to which we shall return in a later chapter.

But to continue.

Prov. xxii. 21. That thou mayest make known words of
              truth,
                 To carry back words to him that sendeth
                 thee.

A. Intro. i. 5. To be able to reply to the speech of him that
              speaketh ;
              6. To make a report to him who sendeth.[2]

---

[1] See Gesenius-Kautzsch, §134, iii. 3.
[2] Griffith renders :

' Knowledge how to answer a statement to its pronouncer,
And return a report to him that has sent him.'

First, as to the Hebrew text; this reads lit. ' For
thee to make known truth, words of truth, to carry
back words, truth to him that sendeth thee.' The
text is quite obviously corrupt, although one would
hardly think so from the R.V. rendering. In the
first line the first ' truth ' is an Aramaic word (*kasht*) [1];
this was probably the marginal note of an Aramaic-
speaking scribe which got into the text by mistake.
In the second line ' truth ' is again inserted (this time
in Hebrew); clearly this was erroneously repeated
from the preceding clause. But even when one has
obtained what may well be regarded as a correct
text, the meaning of the second clause is still quite
uncertain; for when it says, ' to carry back words,'
by whom are they brought ? And who is it that sends
him ? One can give various answers; but the words
are too indefinite to make one feel confidence in the
correctness of the answers which are given by commentators. But it is just this indefiniteness which
is interesting, because it shows that in this case, at
any rate, the compiler of Proverbs, or he who was
the author of the source used by that compiler, copied
directly from the ' Teaching of Amen-em-ope '; for
in the Egyptian book these words are not written in
reference to any particular person or to any particular
circumstance; they are quite general. This passage
occurs in the introductory chapter to the book, in
which the writer enumerates the objects for which it
was written; and among those objects is that one
might learn how, on being sent on a commission, to
bring back a correct report to him by whom he was
sent. It would be interesting to know why this object
and the preceding one were copied, and the far more
important ones ignored, such as teaching on conduct
of life, instruction on well-being (*i.e.* how to attain
it), to guide one on the way of life (in a spiritual sense),

---

[1] קְשֹׁט, cp. Dan. ii. 47; iv. 34.

to practise introspection, and to guide the heart away from evil.   These, one feels, might have appealed more to a Hebrew sage.

Prov. xxii. 22. Rob not the poor because he is poor,
And oppress not the lowly in the gate.
A. II. iv. 4. Beware of robbing the poor,
5. And of oppressing the weak.[1]

Here the two are practically identical ; and both are perfectly straightforward.

Prov. xxii. 23.   This is a very natural addition to the preceding verse for a Hebrew sage ; there is nothing in Amen-em-ope corresponding to it.

Prov. xxii. 24. Be not friendly with one given to anger,
And go not with a passionate man.
A. IX. xi. 13. Consort not with a passionate man,
14. And press not thyself upon him [2] with talk.

The repetition in Proverbs is somewhat jejune ; there is more point in Amen-em-ope's couplet.   Still, the relationship between the two is clear ; one only wonders why the second line in the latter finds no place in the former.

Prov. xxii. 25. Lest he learn thy ways,
To take thy soul with a snare.[3]
A. IX. xi. 15. Guard thy tongue from answering thy superior,
16. And beware of reviling him ;
17. For he is able to ensnare thee with his words,[4]
18. (Therefore) give not free rein to thine answer.[5]

---

[1] See above, p. 22.
[2] Griffith : ' Nor approach him for conversation.'
[3] Reading with Gressmann (in a private communication) :
‎פֶּן יֶאֱלַף אֹרְחֹתֶיךָ לָקַחַת בְּמוֹקֵשׁ לְנַפְשֶׁךָ (cp. Ps. xxxi. 14 (13 in E.V.)).
[4] Griffith renders this line : ' Cause him not to cast his speech to lasso thee.'
[5] This is Griffith's rendering.

It is, of course, only the last two lines which offer the parallel. But with this and the preceding passage in Amen-em-ope there is an interesting parallel in Ben-Sira (Ecclus. viii. 15) :

> Go not with a fierce [1] man,
> Lest evils overwhelm thee ;
> For he will do according to his will, [2]
> And thou wilt perish through his foolishness.

Prov. xxii. 26, 27 have no parallels in Amen-em-ope. The next two parallels, while running consecutively in Proverbs, are again from different parts of the Egyptian book.

Prov. xxii. 28. Remove not the ancient landmark,
    Which thy fathers set up.
A. VI. vii. 12. Remove not the landmark from the bounds
    of the field.

For what follows in the Egyptian text see Prov. xxiii. 10, 11, which is a variant of xxii. 28. The first line in the two passages before us shows their relationship : the reference to ' thy fathers ' in Proverbs would be a very natural addition for a Hebrew.

Prov. xxii. 29. A man that is skilful [3] in his work
    Shall stand before kings.
A. XXX. xxvii. 16, 17 :
    A scribe who is skilful [4] in his office,
    Findeth himself worthy to be a courtier.

In the Hebrew, ' seest thou ' overloads the line. All the verses in this section contain only two lines, so that the third line [5] which the Hebrew has is, in all probability, not an original part of the text. Gressmann

---

[1] Hebr. אָכְזָר ; see Job xli. 2 (xli. 10 in E.V.) = ' passionate.'
[2] Lit. ' For he will go straight before his face.'
[3] This word (māhîr) is used in Ezra vii. 6 in reference to a scribe ; see also Ps. xlv. 1 (2 in Hebr.).
[4] Griffith : ' experienced.'
[5] ' He shall not stand before mean (or obscure) men.'

regards it as 'a correction of the republican period after the Exile,' and there is much to be said for this view.

In the passage under consideration Amen-em-ope is speaking of a scribe, who, if skilful in his calling, may be called upon to exercise some function at court ; it is probable that in the parallel passage in Proverbs where 'a man' is spoken of it is a scribe of whom the writer is thinking ; at any rate, if in Egypt it was normal for a scribe to appear at court, this was certainly also the case among the Jews ; for Ben-Sira, in writing about the scribe, says that :

> He seeketh out the hidden things of proverbs,
> And is conversant with the dark things of parables ;
> He serveth among great men,
> And appeareth before a ruler.   (Ecclus. xxxix. 3, 4.) [1]

See further, for the functions of a scribe, p. 76.

In the next parallel the passages run consecutively in both books.

Prov. xxiii. 1. When thou sittest to eat with a ruler,
　　　　　　　　　Mark well who is before thee ;
　　　　　　2. And put a knife to thy throat,
　　　　　　　　　If thou be a man of great appetite.
　　　　　　3. Desire not his dainties,
　　　　　　　　　Seeing it is deceitful food.

A. XXIII. xxiii. 13–18 :
　　　　　　　　Eat not in the presence of a ruler,
　　　　　　　　And do not (stretch out (?)) thy mouth
　　　　　　　　　towards . . .[2]
　　　　　　　　When thou art replenished with that to
　　　　　　　　　which thou hast no right.[3]

---

[1] So the Greek (the Hebrew is not extant) ; the Syriac, in verse 4, has, more fully : ' In the midst of the powerful he goeth, and in the midst of kings and of great ones he serveth.'

[2] This line is uncertain ; Griffith renders it : ' Nor apply thy mouth at the beginning ' (i.e. of the feast) ; cp. the passage from Ben-Sira quoted below.

[3] Griffith : ' (with) false munchings.'

It is only a delight to thy spittle ;
Look upon the dish [1] that is before thee,
And let that (alone) supply thy need.

While there are considerable varieties in these two
passages, there can be no doubt that, in essence, the
sense is the same in both.   In the first line of Amen-
em-ope's text the negative must have got in by mistake,
as all the succeeding lines show.[2]   In the Hebrew
passage, ' put a knife to thy throat ' is a figurative
expression meaning that self-restraint in eating is to
be exercised.   The word for ' knife ' (sakkîn) does not
occur elsewhere in the Old Testament [3] ;   on its use
at meals, however, see Krauss, *Talmudische Archä-
ologie*, iii. 53, 264, in reference, it is true, to later
times.

The ' deceitful food ' of verse 3 is well illustrated
by a proverb which Wildeboer quotes from Fleischer,
Ali's Hundert Sprüche, pp. 71, 104 : ' The dainties of
a king burn the lips ' (*Die Sprüche*, p. 66 (1897)).

It is worth while quoting in this connexion another
passage from Ben-Sira, for it offers here and there a
better parallel with Amen-em-ope than Proverbs,
when carefully compared :

My son, if thou sittest at the table of a great one,
Open not thy mouth (lit. throat) upon it.
Say not ' There is plenty upon it.'
Remember that an envious (lit. evil) eye is an evil
        thing . . .[4]

---

[1] Griffith : ' cup.'

[2] Griffith (in a private communication) says : ' the vetitive is as
clear as daylight, and cannot be avoided.'

[3] Gressmann would emend the text by reading שִׂשִׂי בִּלְעֶךָ for
שַׂכִּין בְּלֹעֶךָ ; the mention of ' delight,' though only temporary, making
a verbal parallel with Amen-em-ope ; but this would make the verse in
Proverbs somewhat out of harmony with the context, and would
not really improve the parallelism, so far as the general sense is
concerned.

[4] The rest of this verse (13) is parenthetical, and not part of the
original text ; and the verse which follows has got out of place.

Stretch not out thine hand at that at which he (*i.e.* thy
   neighbour) looketh,
And reach not thine hand with his into the dish ;
Eat like a man that which is set before thee,
And eat not greedily lest thou be despised.

(Ecclus. xxxi. (xxxiv.) 12–16.) [1]

The next two passages run again consecutively in
both books :

Prov. xxiii. 4. Toil not to become rich,
   And cease from thy plundering ; [2]
5. Thine eye considereth it diligently, [3]
   And it is not ;
   For it hath surely made for itself wings,
   As an eagle that flieth heavenwards.

A. VII. ix. 14. Toil not after riches,
15. When thy needs are made sure to thee. [4]
16. If stolen goods are brought to thee,
17. They remain not over the night with thee ;
18. At daybreak they are no more in thine
   house.
19. One seeth where they were, but they are not
   (there).
20. The earth hath opened its mouth . . . and
   hath swallowed them ; [5]

x. 1. They are drowned in the underworld. [6]
2. (Or) they have made them a great hole,
   which befits them, [7]
3. They are sunk in the treasure-house. [8]
4. (Or) they have made for themselves wings
   like geese,
5. And have flown into the heavens.

[1] This passage is from the Hebrew, not from the Greek version
from which the R.V. comes.
[2] Reading מִבְּנָתְךָ (Sellin) for מִבִּינָתְךָ.
[3] תִּתְבּוֹגֵן עֵינֶךָ (Gressmann).
[4] *I.e.* when thou hast all thou needest.
[5] Griffith : ' It adjusts it and swallows it.'
[6] Griffith : ' And has sunk them in Tei ' (= the underworld).
[7] Griffith : ' of their measure.'
[8] Griffith : ' corn-store.'

These two passages are clearly identical in thought, much as they differ in detail. The relationship between them strikes one at once; it is only a question as to whether Proverbs is a compression of Amen-em-ope, or Amen-em-ope an expansion of Proverbs, or whether there is a *tertium quid*. For the present we must leave this.

The Hebrew text of Proverbs is in considerable disorder, and two of the lines do not make sense as they stand, or at least not good sense; hence the suggested emendations.

Regarding the ' geese ' mentioned towards the close of the Amen-em-ope passage, Erman points out that the Egyptians sometimes kept a goose even as a pet.[1]

Prov. xxiii. 6. Eat not the bread of him that hath an evil
eye ;
And desire not his dainties.
A. XI. xiv. 5. Covet not the goods of the small man,[2]
6. And hunger not after his bread.

In Prov. xxiii. 7, the first line of which is corrupt, it is somewhat doubtful whether there is a parallelism with what follows in Amen-em-ope; moreover, some of the words in this latter seem to be very uncertain here. It is, therefore, perhaps better to pass over this verse until the experts can give us a more certain rendering of what presumably corresponds to it in the Egyptian book.

Prov. xxiii. 8. The morsel thou hast eaten thou wilt vomit
up,
And wilt lose thy pleasant things.[3]

---

[1] Erman, *Aegypten* (2nd ed. pp. 271, 531).
[2] Griffith : ' dependent.'
[3] Omitting דְּבָרֶיךָ (Gressmann) ; the reference is to what has been eaten.

A. XI. xiv. 17. Thou swallowest too large a mouthful which
thou bringest up again,

18. And thus thou losest thy pleasant (food).[1]

At first sight there seems to be a contrast between
the 'morsel' in the one passage and the 'mouthful'
in the other; but this is not so. The Hebrew word
translated 'morsel' does not mean what we understand by this; it is used several times in reference to
a meal (Gen. xviii. 5; Judges xix. 5, etc.). Uncertain
as some of the sentences in Amen-em-ope are which
precede this passage, there is enough to show that the
words before us are not intended to be understood
in a literal sense; what, in effect, appears to have
been said in what precedes is this: If a man tries to
gain favour with his superior through flattery and
obsequiousness, he will only get curses and the rod
in return; expected favours will turn out to be something very different. It is probable, therefore, that
the whole of the Proverbs passage (verses 6–8) is to
be taken in a figurative sense, but that a copyist, not
realising this, altered some words in the text with a
view to making it more intelligible, thereby only
making things worse.

Prov. xxiii. 9. In the ears of a fool speak not,
For he despiseth the wisdom of thy words.

A. XXI. xxii. 11. Empty not what is in thee (in thy mind)
before everyone,

12. And damage not (thereby) thine influence.

There is an inner parallelism here, even though the
outer form is different between the two passages.
But Ben-Sira, in the Hebrew, has a striking parallel:

---

[1] Griffith renders:
  ' The (too) great mouthful of bread, thou swallowest it and
      vomitest it,
  Thou art emptied of thy good.'

Reveal not thy heart to all flesh,
And drive not away from thee prosperity. (Ecclus. xix. 7;
cp. xxvii. 16 ff. and Prov. xxv. 10.)

Prov. xxiii. 10. Remove not the ancient landmark,
And into the fields of orphans enter not ;
11. For their avenger is strong,
He will plead their cause against thee.
A. VI. vii. 12. Remove not the landmark from the bounds
of the field,[1]
13. Nor shift the position of the measuring-
cord.[2]
14. Covet not (even) a cubit of land,
15. And violate not the widow's boundary.
17. He who wrongly appropriates in a field
16. A furrow . . .[3] worn by time,
18. Though he claim it with false oaths,
19. Will yet be taken captive by the might of
the Moon (-god).[4]

The first line in the Proverbs passage occurs, as
we have seen, in xxii. 28. The emendation suggested
by some commentators, who would read 'widow' for
'ancient,' is unnecessary, and is not favoured by the
Egyptian parallel. In the Hebrew the word *Gôël* is
used for 'avenger,' *i.e.* the technical term for the next
of kin, who was bound by the law to redeem his kins-
man's land (Lev. xxv. 25). Toy points out that
'here the supposition is that there is no human *gôël*,
in which case God Himself will act as protector'[5] ;
this is borne out by the Egyptian parallel. The
second line of the first couplet in Amen-em-ope, which
presents much difficulty to experts, ought, according

---

[1] Griffith : ' on the boundaries of the sown.'
[2] Griffith's rendering.
[3] Griffith : ' The rut of trampling (?).'
[4] Griffith renders these two lines :
' (If) he snare by false oaths,
Is lassoed by the Power of the Moon,' *i.e.* Thoth.
[5] *Op. cit.*, p. 432.

to the Proverbs parallel, to contain a prohibition against interfering with the orphan's plot; this would correspond well with the second couplet. Lange thinks that the line, ' a furrow . . . worn by time,' the meaning of which is uncertain (see Griffith's rendering, note 3), may perhaps refer to a foot-path. ' In Egypt,' he says, ' owing to the general coveting of land, the foot-paths between the plots became ever narrower because everyone tried to grab for himself part of his neighbour's land.'

Here the parallels cease; the Egyptian book offers nothing which can be paralleled with the last three verses of this collection in Proverbs.

The question as to what is to be gathered from the fact of these parallels will be dealt with in the concluding chapter

CHAPTER V

THE religious atmosphere pervading Amen-em-ope's book demands that it should be studied not only from the point of view of a ' Wisdom ' book but also from that of a book of religious teaching in the stricter sense. For this purpose it must be read in the light of some other Old Testament writings.[1] A detailed comparison between Amen-em-ope's religious ideas and those of the Old Testament is, of course, out of the question here, our object being merely to indicate the interest of such a study. And our concern is not primarily to find literary parallels, though these occur, but rather to show that there existed a community of religious thought in some essentials among the peoples of the Oriental world of those days. How far we are justified in seeing the influence of one religious system on the other is a difficult question ; but we shall devote a few words to this in the concluding chapter.

I. *The Book of Deuteronomy*

There are good grounds for the belief that the Book of Deuteronomy emanated from scribal-prophetical, not

---

[1] Were it not that the subject would take us too far afield, various products of Babylonian religious literature ought to be taken into consideration in this connexion. Reference may, however, be made to G. R. Driver's admirable essay, ' The Psalms in the light of Babylonian research ' in the volume edited by Canon D. C. Simpson, *The Psalmists*, pp. 109–175 (1926).

priestly, circles.[1] If this was so, it is an important and significant fact in the present connexion. For the scribes, in the wide sense of the word, occupied positions of great influence at Court, both in Egypt and Israel, and doubtless in other countries too. Being skilled in the art of writing, they held, of necessity, the posts of Government officials, and would have, therefore, to conduct the affairs of State generally. There is also good evidence that they travelled on diplomatic business to the courts of other lands ; so that the scribes of different countries had opportunities of coming into contact with one another. Moreover, among their number were those who were authors and literary experts, as we know. Amen-em-ope was, as we have seen, a scribe ; there would, therefore, be a kindred feeling and a community of interests between him and those who belonged to a similar class in other countries. If, then, Deuteronomy came from scribal circles, there would be an initial point of contact between it and the ' Teaching of Amen-em-ope.' That, of course, does not settle the question of the nature of the relationship between the two, supposing that it exists ; but it makes any parallels between them the more interesting.

Obviously we should not look for parallels with Amen-em-ope in most of the legal detail in Deuteronomy ; [2] for each was written with an entirely different purpose. But what is worthy of note is that the two funda-mental and outstanding features of each should, in essence, be similar.

We have seen, in dealing with the religious stand-point of Amen-em-ope (Chap. II.), what an exalted conception of the Deity he sets forth ; and how he insists upon the duty of man to man ; and how the

---

[1] See, e.g. *Zeitschrift für die A. T. Wissenschaft*, pp. 146 f. (1925).
[2] We are thinking more especially of the kernel of Deuteronomy, Chaps. v.-xxvi. and xxviii.

motive-power impelling to right living and deterring
from what is evil is the sense of the divine which
permeates his book. This religious atmosphere is
similar to that of the Book of Deuteronomy. It is
unnecessary to describe in any detail the Deuteronomic
religious ideas here ; this has been done often enough
elsewhere.[1]

There were special factors which contributed towards
the formulation of the Deuteronomist's doctrine of
God. He laid especial stress on the unity of God
because of the prevalence of the worship of other
gods ; he taught the love and faithfulness of God
because this had been illustrated by His having brought
the Israelites out of Egypt, and settled them in their
permanent home in the Promised Land. He taught
the righteousness and ethical character of God in order
to explain to his people the necessity of divine visita-
tion in the event of unfaithfulness to His ethical
requirements. Whatever it was that lay behind
Amen-em-ope's formulation of his doctrine of God, it
was quite different from this. Yet in each book there
is this high conception of God ; and in a number of
ways the conceptions are similar, even identical, in
each. In addition to this, we have not only a similarity
in the way in which the duty of man to his fellow-
creatures is inculcated, but there is also the fact that
the intention and motive are the same, viz. what
may be called the *Godward view* ; the doing of an act
for the sake of God, and not only because it is a
kindness to a fellow-man.

These are facts which are of prime importance,
and of great interest in comparing the religious thought
of the two books.

There are also some parallels of the more ordinary
kind to which attention is worth drawing. Amen-em-ope,

---

[1] Nowhere better than by S. R. Driver, *Deuteronomy* (Inter-
national Crit. Com.), pp. xix. ff. (1902).

in various passages in his book, speaks of things which
are ' an abomination to God ' (*e.g.* in Chaps. X.,
XIII., and elsewhere). This expression is frequent
in Deuteronomy ; it occurs, among other passages,
in xvii. 1 ; xviii. 12 ; xxii. 5 ; xxiii. 18 ; xxv. 16.
It is, of course, the thought expressed—always in
reference to some sin—not the expression itself, which
is noteworthy.

Among passages in which there is parallelism of
thought the following may be cited as examples :

Deut. xii. 19. Take heed to thyself that thou forsake not
the Levite as long as thou livest upon thy
land.
A. V. vi. 16. Remove not a servant of God,
17. In order to benefit another.

Both passages show a solicitude for servants of the
temple *personnel* that they may receive their due.

Deut.   xvi.   19. Thou shalt not wrest judgement ; thou
shalt not respect persons.
Neither shalt thou take a gift . . . (see
also xxiv. 17).
A. XX. xx. 21. Bring no man into misfortune in a court
of justice,
22. And disturb not the just man.
xxi. 1. Be not influenced by fine clothes
2. And refuse not him that is in rags.[1]
3. Receive no gift from one who is powerful,
4. And oppress not the poor for his benefit.

Deut.   xix.   14. Thou shalt not remove thy neighbour's
landmark
That they of old time have set.
A. VI. vii. 12. Remove not the landmark at the boundary of the field.

---

[1] On this passage see note on p. 42.

Deut. xix. 18, 19. . . . If the witness be a false witness, and hath testified falsely against his brother, then shall ye do unto him as he had thought to do unto his brother.

A. XIII. xvi. 1. Be not a witness with false words.[1]
2. And turn not aside [2] another by means of thy tongue.

Deut. xxiii. 15. Thou shalt not deliver unto his master a servant which is escaped from his master unto thee.

A. VIII. xi. 6, 7. Cry not ' crime ' at a man ; Hide the manner of (a fugitive's) flight.

Deut. xxiv. 14, 15. Thou shalt not oppress an hired servant that is poor and needy . . . in his day thou shalt give him his hire ; neither shall the sun go down upon it ; for he is poor and setteth his heart upon it (see also xv. 7, 8).

A. II. iv. 4. Beware of robbing the poor,
5. And of oppressing the weak.[3]

Deut. xxiv. 19, 21. When thou reapest thine harvest in the field, and hast forgot a sheaf in the field, thou shalt not go again to fetch it ; it shall be for the stranger, for the fatherless and for the widow. . . .

A. XXVIII. xxvi. 9–12. Here there is a reference to the widow who gathers the fallen ears of corn in the field,[4] and an admonition to show kindness to the stranger. Although differing in detail, it is probable that the thought in each passage is the same, viz. not to refuse the remnants of the harvest to

---

[1] Griffith : ' Bear not witness by a false statement.'
[2] Griffith : ' Nor displace . . .'
[3] See note on p. 22.
[4] See Lange, *op. cit.*, p. 130.

widows and orphans, and to show consideration to the stranger.

Deut. xxv. 13-15. Thou shalt not have in thy bag divers weights, a great and a small. Thou shalt not have in thine house divers measures, a great and a small. A perfect and just weight shalt thou have ; a perfect and just measure shalt thou have.

A. XVI. xvii. 18. Move not the scales, and falsify not the weights ;

                19. And diminish not the parts of the corn-measure. . . .

                22. Thoth [1] sitteth beside the scales,

xvii. 1. And his heart is its plummet.[2] . . .

                4. Make not weights for thyself which are too light. . . .

Deut. xxvii. 18. Cursed be he that maketh the blind to wander out of the way (cp. Lev. xix. 14).

A. XXV. xxiv. 9. Laugh not at a blind man.

These will suffice. In bringing forward these points of similarity of religious thought between the Book of Deuteronomy and the Egyptian sage, it is not intended to suggest that the latter was influenced by the former ; a book which is so anti-Egyptian as Deuteronomy is, would not, in any case, have been regarded with favour by an Egyptian—supposing he had ever come across it. What is suggested is the possibility that the spirit and teaching which produced the Book of Deuteronomy had also some influence upon the thought of circles to which such men as

---

[1] Lit. ' The Ape,' one of the animals in which Thoth, the inventor of balance and weights, was believed to manifest himself (Lange).

[2] The plummet of the Egyptian scales was often made in the form of a heart (Ranke).

Amen-em-ope belonged. Gressmann [1] has shown conclusively how widespread were certain elements of 'Wisdom' all over the East, and how from the time of Solomon onwards extraneous influences in this domain are to be discerned in various parts of the Old Testament. The existence of the interchange of thought may, therefore, be regarded as proved. The question is whether Israelite thinkers were always receivers only, and not sometimes imparters. In the religious domain Israel developed in spiritual conception from the middle of the eighth century B.C. onwards in a degree which vastly outstripped that of the religious teachers of other nations. With the manifold means of communication and intercourse which are known to have existed, is it not possible, nay probable, that receptive minds among other nations, and perhaps among those in Egypt especially, may have absorbed some of the exalted ideas of Israelite belief, which they must have recognised as being superior to anything hitherto experienced by them ? That is a question which, we feel, must be answered in the affirmative.

II. *The Book of Psalms*

What has been said is not illustrated by the Book of Deuteronomy only ; the Psalms are also worth considering in this connexion. And here again it is not so much a question of parallel passages as the conception of God, His attributes, and His relationship to men, together with man's duty to man, in which there is community of thought with the Egyptian sage.

---

[1] In the Essay referred to above in the *Zeitschrift für die alttestamentliche Wissenschaft* for 1924, pp. 282 ff.

G

In reading the summary of Amen-em-ope's religious
standpoint given above (Chap. II.) thought-parallels
with the Psalms soon suggest themselves ; but it is
well worth giving a few concrete examples.

In Amen-em-ope I. iii. 13, there is the figurative
expression, ' the casket of thy belly ' ; both expression
and idea are uncommon ; but in Ps. xvii. 14, very
different as the connexion is, there is nevertheless the
idea of the ' belly ' as a receptacle of treasure.

Again, in III. v. 15-17 the sage bids his disciple
withdraw himself from the passionate man when
following his characteristic tendencies, for God knows
how to deal with him. The passage runs according
to Griffith's rendering :

> v. 15. The passionate man in his hour,—
> 16. Withdraw thyself from him ;
> Leave him to his own devices,
> 17. God will know how to reply to him.

The expression ' in his hour,' meaning ' when his
characteristic tendencies are stirred,' is a frequent
expression in Egyptian (Griffith). There is much the
same thought contained in Ps. xxxvii. 7-9 :

Fret not thyself because of him who prospereth in his way,
Because of the man that doeth evil devices.
Cease from anger, and forsake wrath . . .
For evil-doers shall be cut off.

The words ' cease from anger, and forsake wrath '
(lit. ' heat ') may reasonably be understood as of
withdrawing from the passionate man ; and that the
cutting-off of evil-doers is God's act (= ' God will
know how to reply to him ') is implied in the context.
It is, therefore, quite possible that one or other of
these two writers inspired the other, who then put the
thought in a form which appealed to him.

In the same Psalm, v. 16, there is a further example of this :

> Better is a little that the righteous hath
> Than the abundance of many wicked.

Similar to this are Amen-em-ope's words (VI. ix. 5, 6) :

> Better is poverty (or, the poor man) in the hand of God
> Than wealth in the store-house.

' In the hand of God ' here obviously signifies something different from what the phrase means in XXV. xxiv. 11.

There is conceivably another verse in this Psalm which likewise witnesses to a community of thought. Amen-em-ope says in XXI. xxii. 7, 8 :

> Place thyself in the arms of God.[1]
> Thy silence [2] will overthrow them.

The reference here is to what a man should do when there is danger of an enemy. In Ps. xxxvii. 1 there is a similar sentence to that just quoted : ' Fret not thyself because of evil-doers,' showing that the thought is of enemies ; and in verse 5 comes the thought similar to that of Amen-em-ope :

> Commit [3] thy way unto Jahweh,
> And trust in him, and he will do it.
>   (Cp. xxiii. 8, Hebr. 9.)

Much more striking, however, than these is the following parallel ; the passage in Amen-em-ope is IV. vi. 1–12 :

> 1. The passionate man in the temple,
> 2. He is like a tree that groweth in the forest ;
> 3. In one moment it loseth its branches,
> 4. And it findeth its end in (. . .) ; [4]

---

[1] Griffith renders the line : ' Sit thee down at the hands of God.'
[2] Griffith : ' Thy tranquillity.'   [3] Lit. ' Roll.'
[4] Griffith renders this line : ' Its end is reached in the dockyard (?)';
Erman and Lange render the last word ' harbour,' Ranke does not translate it.

5. It is swept [1] away from its place,
6. And the flame is its burial. [2]
7. But the truly silent one, when he standeth aside,
8. He is like a tree that groweth in a plot. [3]
9. It groweth green, and the fruit thereof increaseth,
10. It standeth in the presence of its Lord ;
11. Its fruits are sweet, its shade is pleasant,
12. And it findeth its end in the garden.

The thought of the first six lines seems to be that the passionate man is like a tree growing in the forest, which is quickly hewn down, stripped of its branches, and conveyed to the harbour (or dockyard) ; there it is loaded on board a ship which sails away to its destination ; ultimately the trunk is used for fire-wood. This may or may not be the meaning ; but, in any case, there is intended to be a great contrast between this tree and the one that grows in a garden.

The closeness of thought between what is said here and the Psalmist's picture in Ps. i. will be seen to be very striking ; in the latter the godly man is first spoken of, and then the wicked, and the imagery is also a little different ; but this does not affect the general similarity of the metaphor in each :

Blessed is the man that walketh not in the counsel of the
    wicked. . . .
He shall be like a tree planted by the streams of water,
That bringeth forth its fruit in its season,
Whose leaf also doth not wither ;
And whatsoever he doeth shall prosper.
The wicked are not so ;
But are like the chaff which the wind driveth away.

The contrast in Amen-em-ope is between the 'passionate man' and the 'silent one.' The former figures often in the book, and is perhaps equivalent to the 'wrathful man' in Prov. xv. 18 ; xxii. 24

---

[1] Griffith : ' floated.'   [2] Griffith : ' winding sheet.'
[3] Griffith : ' in a plot,' a different word from ' garden.'

(cp. xxix. 22), or the ' wicked' as in Ps. i. ; Gressmann thinks the Hebrew *ra'*, ' the evil man,' is the
equivalent.   The antithesis to this ' passionate man '
is the ' silent one ' ; he is not often mentioned in the
book, but the expression is a well-known one, and
occurs in other Egyptian writings, says Lange, who
gives this instance : ' I have been a silent (or tranquil)
one (" *gr* ") since I came forth from the womb.'   From
what is said in Chap. V of Amen-em-ope's book about
this type of man it is clear that he represented the
religious, saintly character ; he would thus be equivalent to the *Zaddik*, or ' righteous ' (cp. Ps. i. 6), or
possibly the *Chassid* or ' pious ' one (cp. Prov. ii. 8).
Lange says that the ' silent ' one is he who associates
the ideas of silence and the truth, and that this type
of godly man is the central idea of Amen-em-ope's
preaching.   ' In the presence of its Lord ' implies
the presence of the ' silent one ' in the temple ; ' Lord '
has the determinative of a god, which is always the
case in texts like this (Griffith).

In reference to this passage Blackman says that
' the Egyptian origin of this simile is made the more
certain by the appearance of another instance of
Egyptian influence ' in the next verse of the Psalm :

Therefore the wicked shall not stand in the judgement
   (v. 5).

' the only occurrence in the Psalms of any reference
to the posthumous judgement, and one of the reasons
for critics hitherto assigning this Psalm to the third
century B.C.   A third possible trace of Egyptian
influence in Ps. i.,' he continues, ' is to be found in
the words of verse 2 :

And in his law doth he meditate day and night.

' Are they reminiscent of the exhortations addressed
to would-be scribes that occur more than once in

Egyptian school-texts of the XIX and XX dynasties,
" Give heed to writing by day and read by night " ? ' [1]

This last parallel is distinctly interesting ; but it
must not be pressed, for the study of the Law had
from the time of Ezra been the main pre-occupation
of the Jews ; and one can see from such passages as
Ps. cxix. 97, 148, 164, that the thought of studying the
Law night and day was a familiar one to the devout Jew.

In connexion with the first passage quoted in Ps. i.
Gressmann points to Jer. xvii. 5–8, where the parallel
with Amen-em-ope is in some respects even closer :

> (Cursed is the man that trusteth in man, and maketh
> flesh his arm, and whose heart departeth from Jahweh) :

then comes the parallel :

> For he shall be like a tamarisk in the desert, and shall
> not see when good cometh ; but shall inhabit the
> parched places in the wilderness, a salt land and not
> inhabited. Blessed is the man that trusteth in Jah-
> weh, and whose hope Jahweh is. For he shall be as
> a tree planted by the waters and that spreadeth out
> her roots by the river, and shall not fear when the heat
> cometh, but his leaf shall be green ; and shall not be
> careful in the year of drought, neither shall cease from
> yielding fruit.

This must have been written about three centuries
before Ps. i. was penned ; did the prophet borrow the
simile from Amen-em-ope ? It by no means follows
necessarily. Both may have utilised material the
origin of which is to be sought in fables about trees
and plants which came from the ancient Babylonians.[2]

We come next to a comparison between two
passages which do not, at first sight, give one the idea
of parallelism ; but on closer examination it will be

---

[1] In his essay in *The Psalmists*, p. 195.
[2] See the references given in Gressmann's essay already referred
to, p. 283.

seen that there is a good deal of community of thought between the two. The Amen-em-ope passage is V. vii. 7–10 :

7. All the silent ones [1] in the temple—
8. They say : ' Great is Rê in rewarding.' [2]
9. Hold fast to the silent ones [1] and thou wilt find life,
10. And thy body shall prosper upon earth.

With this compare Ps. xxii. 25, 26 (26, 27 in Hebr.) :

Of thee cometh my praise in the great congregation,
My vows will I pay before them that fear him.
The meek shall eat and be satisfied ;
They that praise Jahweh are they that seek him.
Let their [3] heart live for ever.

The parallelism lies in these points :

The scene is laid in the house of worship, ' in the temple ' = ' in the great congregation.' The praise of God figures in each ; ' Great is Rê ' = ' Of thee cometh my praise,' and ' they that praise Jahweh.' The association of the godly among themselves : ' hold fast to the silent ones ' = ' my vows will I pay before them that fear him.' The prosperity of the godly : ' thou wilt find life, and thy body shall prosper upon earth ' = ' the meek shall eat and be satisfied,' ' let their heart live for ever.'

Different as the forms of expression are in each writer, it is difficult to believe that the identity of thought in all these particulars can be fortuitous. It is also worth pointing out that in the line immediately preceding the passage in Amen-em-ope there occurs an Egyptianised Semitic word (*mikmereth* ' net '), used also in the Old Testament (Job i. 15). It is an interesting point ; nevertheless, it must be

---

[1] Lange : ' humble ' or ' modest ' ones ; Griffith ' tranquil man.'
[2] Griffith : ' Great is the good pleasure of Rê.'   He says that ' the sentiment is submission to the will of Rê.'
[3] Following the Septuagint.

acknowledged that this is not *necessarily* significant, for the word may have been taken over into the Egyptian language before the Hebrews, as a nation, were settled in Canaan.[1]

The next example is again one which does not at first appear to contain parallel thoughts ; but it is just possible that the Egyptian and the Hebrew thinker are putting forth the same idea, each in his own special way, and from his own point of view. Amen-em-ope in VII. ix. 10–13 says (Griffith's rendering) :

> Cast not thy heart after riches ;
> There is no ignoring of Shay and Renent.
> Place not for thyself thy thoughts (on things) outside ;
> Every man is (destined) for his hour.

Shay and Renent are ' Psais and Termuthis, deities of fortune ' (Griffith) ; paraphrased, the passage may be taken to mean : Be not intent on gaining riches ; there is a higher power, not to be ignored, on whose will the possession of wealth depends ; therefore do not concentrate thy thoughts on these external things, for every man possesses only what the higher power accords him.

This thought is, in effect, precisely what is expressed in Ps. lxii. 10–12 (Hebr. 11–13) :

> If riches increase, set not your heart (thereon) ;
> Once hath God spoken, twice have I heard this,
> That ' power belongeth unto God ' ;
> And unto thee, O Lord, belongeth mercy,
> For thou renderest to man according to his work.

Once more, in Amen-em-ope VII. x. 12–15 it is said :

> Pray to the sun [2] when he riseth,
> And say : ' Grant me prosperity and health ' ;
> Then will he give thee thy needs for thy life,
> And thou wilt be free [3] from fear.

---

[1] See further below, p. 98.   [2] Lit. *Atēn*, the solar disc.
[3] Griffith : ' safe.'

It may well be that the Hebrew religious poet, on reading this, expressed the thought in his own way in saying :

> For sun and shield is Jahweh, (our) God,
> Grace and glory giveth Jahweh ;
> He withholdeth not good from them that walk uprightly ;
> O Jahweh of hosts, blessed is the man that trusteth in thee.   (Ps. lxxxiv. 11, 12, Hebr. 12, 13.)

In this case it is interesting to note that the thought-parallelism runs line by line in each passage.

One other passage may be quoted to show that Amen-em-ope expresses a thought which is often a theme in the Psalmists, namely, the untimely fate which will ultimately overtake the wicked. In VI. viii. 1–8 he says :

> viii. 1. Mark him that doeth such things on earth,
>   2. He is the enemy [1] of the weak,
>   3. He is an adversary working destruction within thee ; [2]
>   4. Deprival of life is in his eye ; [3]
>   5. His house is an enemy to the city,
>   6. His barns shall be destroyed,
>   7. His possessions shall be taken from the hand of his children,
>   8. And his property shall be given to another.[4]

While there is no parallel to this in the Psalms, there are many passages which contain the thought, *e.g.* lxxiii. 18, 19 ; xcii. 6 ff. (7 ff. in Hebr.) ; xciv. 20 ff. ; cix. 6 ff. ; cxl. 6 ff. (10 ff. in Hebr.), and others.

---

[1] Griffith : ' oppressor.'

[2] So Griffith. Erman and Ranke render : ' Who is ruined within himself ' (lit. ' in his belly ' ; Ranke says in a note that the text has erroneously got ' in thy '). Lange agrees with Griffith.

[3] So Griffith. Erman and Ranke render : ' Life is taken away from his eye.' Lange : ' He takes away life through his eye.'

[4] In lines 6–8 Griffith has the verbs in the perfect.

Finally, there are two further parallels [1] with Amen-em-ope in other Biblical books ; these must be quoted, for they help towards forming conclusions regarding the whole subject of these parallelisms.

The Amen-em-ope passage has already been dealt with in another connexion ; it is in Chap. XXV :

> Man is clay and straw
> And God is his builder.

The thought of the first line occurs in Job iv. 19 :

> . . . How much more them that dwell in houses of clay,
> Whose foundation is in the dust,
> Which are crushed like the moth !

Amen-em-ope continues :

> He destroyeth and buildeth up daily,
> He maketh a thousand small according to his will,
> And he maketh a thousand to be princes. . . .

In 1 Sam. ii. 6–8 we have a close parallelism of thought :

> Jahweh killeth and maketh alive,
> He bringeth down to Sheol, and bringeth up.
> Jahweh maketh poor, and maketh rich :
> He bringeth low, he also lifteth up.
> He raiseth up the poor out of the dust.
> He lifteth up the needy from the dunghill.
> He maketh them to sit with princes. . . .
> (Cp. Ps. lxxv. 7, Hebr. 8.)

Finally, in Amen-em-ope I. iii. 15 the expression ' hurricane of words ' (Griffith : ' gale of speech ') recalls the thought in Job viii. 2 :

> How long wilt thou speak these things,
> And the words of thy mouth be a mighty wind ?

It will thus be seen from the passages quoted in this and the preceding chapter—and they are by no

[1] We are indebted to Gressmann for these ; p. 279 in his essay.

means exhaustive—that there is much parallelism in thought, and identity of religious atmosphere, between some books of the Hebrew Scriptures and the 'Teaching of Amen-em-ope.' That this latter, a comparatively short book, should show so much affinity with the Old Testament is a fact both remarkable and interesting. What is to be said in face of it ? That must be our next task.

CHAPTER VI

SOME CONCLUDING CONSIDERATIONS

THE whole question of extraneous influences upon the religion and literature of Israel—using the word in a wide sense as embracing the nation as a whole, during the different periods of its history—has received considerable attention in recent times, and small wonder, for numberless archaeological finds, and the discovery and decipherment of Babylonian, Egyptian, and other texts, have thrown much light on the religious beliefs of the ancient peoples of the Near East. The result has been to show the existence of much community of thought and religious conception between Israel and other nations in regard to things which in times past were believed to have been the unique possession of the former.

The book which we have been considering is a striking example of this ; here we get thought-parallels with several Old Testament books, and, in the case of one at least, even verbal parallels. Most of those scholars who have so far studied the matter incline to the belief that we have here simply a case of Jewish writers borrowing from an Egyptian source. No doubt in the past the exact contrary would have been held. But it is doubtful whether either of these two positions really satisfies all the facts of the case. For there are various considerations worth weighing, which seem to justify the contention that while to a very appreciable extent Israel was influenced by Egypt, and borrowed both in thought and, to a far less extent, in word, yet that the influence and the borrowing were mutual ; that the receptiveness among the thinkers of both nations during certain periods of their histories resulted in the enrichment of each.

We are dealing in particular now with the ' Teaching of Amen-em-ope ' and its relation to some of the Old Testament writings. The date of this book bears directly on the question of influence and borrowing as between Israel and Egypt, *i.e.* as to which of the two was the one to exercise influence, and which of the two borrowed.

But for the moment we are thinking not so much of the date of Amen-em-ope's book as of the period during which the relations between Israel and Egypt were such that the likelihood of religious or literary influence of the one on the other might be contemplated.

The earliest period, as we have already seen, during which the nature of the contact between the two peoples was favourable for this was during the reign of Solomon ; and here the influence might have been indirect, through the Phoenicians, or direct, through the friendly relations between the two royal houses. Blackman, in dealing with the subject, says : ' At the end of the XX dynasty [1] Byblos still maintained close trade and cultural relations with Egypt, as can be seen from the " Adventure of Unamun." [2]   In process of time these hymns [*i.e.* hymns composed during the XVIII dynasty], or *motifs* from these hymns, would be taken over and adapted to the natural features of the country by the native Phoenician singers.   These latter may, in their turn, have passed them on to the Hebrews either during the reign of Solomon, when Hiram's workmen built for him the temple of Jahweh at Jerusalem—a building distinctly Egyptian in its plan and in its sacrificial accessories—

[1] *I.e., circa* 1100 B.C.
[2] See Erman, *Die Literatur der Aegypter*, pp. 225 ff. (1923).

or during the reign of Ahab, whose Phoenician wife,
Jezebel, is known to have favoured the introduction
of Phoenician religious and political ideas.' [1] The
reference here is to psalms, but what is said would,
of course, apply equally to religious ideas contained
in other writings. And then there is also the possibility that Egyptian influences may have come in
directly through those who accompanied the Pharaoh's
daughter when she came to Jerusalem to be Solomon's
wife (1 Kings iii. 1).

But, while the possibility is recognised, it must be
held to be improbable that at this period the Israelites
were influenced by Egyptian religious or, at any rate,
literary thought, for the soil was not yet sufficiently
receptive ; moreover, there was not yet among the
Israelites anything that could be called literature.
On the other hand, the Egyptians were in both
domains so very much more advanced that the idea
of Hebrew influence on them is excluded. Nor, for
the same reasons, was the reign of Ahab any more
favourable.

From the point of view of the Old Testament scholar
there can be no question of the influence of Israel's
religion on non-Israelites until the teaching of the
eighth-century prophets had had time to fructify.
On the other hand, if previous to this time the mental
and religious soil of Israel was not yet prepared to
receive the more advanced Egyptian thought, it is
certain that after the prophetical teaching and ideals
had once taken root there was no likelihood of any
Egyptian influence affecting the *religion* of Israel

----

[1] *Op. cit.*, p. 192. In later times also Egypt was in close touch
with Phoenicia ; for example, Psammetichus II, son of Necho, in
591 B.C. ' visited Phoenicia in state, in all probability by sea, apparently on a peaceful progress, as he was accompanied by a retinue of
priests, and took with him " the votive wreaths of Amon." No
doubt this was a purely religious visit or pilgrimage to the ancient
Egyptian shrine at Byblos ' (*Camb. Anc. Hist.*, iii., p. 300).

permanently,[1] whatever may be said of *literary* influence.

In the time of Isaiah, during the reign of Hezekiah, we find a relationship between the Jewish kingdom and Egypt which is very interesting. There is a strong Egyptian party, headed by the king, which is in favour of relying on Egypt in view of the imminent approach of the Assyrians. The Egyptian alliance is vehemently opposed by Isaiah (xxx. 1–17, xxxi.) ; but the intercourse between the two countries persists.

Either at this time, or soon after, the prophet (if not Isaiah, then one of slightly later date), who speaks as a religious rather than as a political leader, utters words in reference to Egypt which are quite of the kind that would be addressed to his own people. The whole of Isa. xix.,[2] ' The burden of Egypt,' is most important in this connexion, and should be read ; a few quotations from it must be given in order to bear out the point it is desired to make. The bulk of this

---

[1] Cp. the Assyrian influence on religion and cult during Manasseh's reign, which were only *transient*.

[2] Many modern commentators regard this chapter, and especially vv. 18–25, as non-Isaianic (verse 18 is obviously a late gloss) ; some hold that these verses belong to the Greek period, mainly on account of its universalistic teaching ; but, in view of the universalism taught by some of the earlier prophets, this late date for the passage does not seem justified. Sellin, in discussing the subject, says : ' The mention of a *mazzēbah* as a well-known feature of the cultus, v. 19, is decidedly in favour of a pre-Deuteronomic date (cp. Deut. xvi. 22). And since the Elephantiné papyri have lately proved that there was a sanctuary in Egypt long before the time of Cambyses, and as it has become almost certain that the colony there had its beginnings as early as the time of Psammetichus (about 650), and vv. 18 ff. accordingly refer entirely to the pre-exilic (cp. Assyria vv. 23 ff.) and pre-Deuteronomic circumstances, it will be advisable to be very cautious in pronouncing a categorical judgement, and to be content for the present with the probability that the first half was written by Isaiah, and the second half about the middle of the seventh century ; it is possible that passages like Hos. ix. 3, xi. 5, Deut. xvii. 16 take us back to the time of Hezekiah, and therefore to that of Isaiah himself '—*Introduction to the Old Testament*, p. 133 (1923).

oracle is a prophecy of coming evil upon Egypt, but, as the sequel shows, the punishment is only a means of purification, the result of which will be to make the Egyptians Jahweh's people. Thus, after the downfall of the country is foretold, it is said in vv. 19 ff.: ' In that day shall there be an altar to Jahweh in the midst of the land of Egypt, and a pillar (*mazzēbah*) at the border thereof to Jahweh. And it shall be for a sign, and for a witness unto Jahweh of hosts in the land of Egypt; for they shall cry unto Jahweh because of the oppressor; and he shall send them a helper who will strive (for them) and deliver them. And Jahweh shall make himself known to Egypt, and the Egyptians shall know Jahweh in that day; yea, they shall worship with sacrifice and oblation, and shall vow a vow unto Jahweh, and perform it. And Jahweh shall smite Egypt, smiting and healing, and they shall return unto Jahweh, and he shall be entreated of them and shall heal them.'

Without going into exegetical details, one thing is clear from this passage, viz. that the prophet contemplated the acceptance of the worship of the God of Israel on the part of Egypt. Such an attitude indicates belief in a mission of Israel as the witness of Jahweh among the Egyptians; and the consciousness of this would obviously result in a need being felt of carrying on propagandist work among those with whom Israel had relations. No people at this time had closer relations with Palestine than the Egyptians; and it must be regarded as probable that in the constant coming and going of Egyptians some among the prophet's followers saw an opportunity of proclaiming belief in Jahweh and his teaching. It was a period during which influences could be both exercised and received.

A little later came the downfall of Assyria, and the revival of Egypt under Psammetichus I (663–609 B.C.), after her bitter experiences (cp. Nah. iii. 8–10) ; these things were not likely to have been without effect in Judah. And, on the other hand, the reform movement in Judah, with the fructifying of prophetical teaching, made it a centre of religious teaching, which may well have impressed thinkers and teachers of other lands, and, above all, of Egypt.

If Israelite religion, then, was to exercise any influence outside the borders of its own land, it could not, for the reasons already stated, have done so previous to the period under consideration ; while, so far as Egypt was concerned, this period was a favourable one for the reception of religious influences.

Now we have seen the uniqueness of Amen-em-ope's religious standpoint in Egyptian literature ; we have also seen how much affinity there is between the religious thought and the ethical teaching of his book and that of various Old Testament books. We are, therefore, led to the conclusion that so far as the *religious* atmosphere of his book is concerned we are justified in seeing the influence of the religion of Israel. We feel the truth of Wallis Budge's words when he writes : ' It appears to me certain that Amen-em-ope's high moral and religious ideals were inspired by an influence that was not of African but of Asiatic origin.' [1]

A further conclusion, which follows from what has been said, is that the ' Teaching of Amen-em-ope ' was written sometime during this period. [2]

The experts, as pointed out above, differ widely as to the date of the original work. There is no doubt, however, that Lange gives more tangible grounds for the comparatively late date for which he contends than do the other authorities for their earlier dates ;

----

[1] *Op. cit.*, p. 221.
[2] There is not necessarily any reason to suppose that the British Museum copy was written long after the original was composed.

H

and Erman and Griffith seem inclined to agree with
him, more or less. Lange's reasons for a comparatively late date are, of course, quite different
from those which we have attempted to give.

Turning now to the question of literary relationship
between Egypt and Israel, there is an important
preliminary consideration for which the present writer
is indebted to Professor Gressmann. In the essay [1]
already several times referred to, he draws attention
to the presence of Semitic loan-words in ancient
Egyptian writings. This had already been noted
by other scholars, but its bearing on the subject under
discussion had escaped me until Gressmann was kind
enough to point it out. He mentioned, for example,
the numerous Canaanite glosses which occur in the
Papyrus Anastasi I,[2] a writing belonging to the time
of Rameses II (about 1340–1273 B.C.). 'These
glosses,' says S. A. Cook, 'together with ancient
place and personal names, and the Semitic words
preserved in Egyptian, present a not inconsiderable
amount of interesting material.' [3] Among these
Semitic words which are closely related to Hebrew
are : *sôpher yode'* (' a knowing,' or skilful, ' scribe ') ;
har (' mountain.') ; *māhîr* (' quick,' or ' apt '), used
of a scribe ; *ne'arin* (' young men ') ; *zaba'* (' host '),
'ari (' lion '), *na'em* (' pleasant '), *kěmo* (' like ').[4] The
presence of Canaanite words in Egyptian writings
shows that as early as the fourteenth century B.C.
Semitic scribes exercised a literary influence on
Egyptian writers. That is a fact well worth bearing

[1] *Die neugefundene Lehre des Amen-em-ope* . . . in ZAtW. pp.
294 ff. (1924).
[2] Erman, *Die Literatur der Aegypter*, pp. 270–294 (1923) ; Gardiner, Egyptian Hieratic Texts I. 1, *The Papyrus Anastasi* (1911).
[3] *Camb. Anc. Hist.*, II. p. 332 (1924).
[4] In Amen-em-ope there are the Hebrew words for ' net ' and
' pure gold ' transcribed, and an Egyptian adaptation of the Hebrew
word for ' where,' see Griffith, *op. cit.*, pp. 203, 211, 215. The word
for ' pure gold ' (כֶּתֶם) occurs in Prov. xxv. 12.

in mind in the present discussion, since from it one may reasonably deduce the existence of a similar influence in later times.

We may note next that various indications in the Old Testament show that the wisdom of the Egyptians was well known among the Israelites.

Thus, in 1 Kings iv. 30, for example, it is said that 'Solomon's wisdom excelled the wisdom of all the children of the East, and all the wisdom of Egypt'; *i.e.* the historian who wished to extol the wisdom which later ages supposed Solomon to have possessed could think of no greater wisdom for him to excel than that of the East and of Egypt. In Isa. xix. 11 ff. the traditional wisdom of Egypt, which is taken for granted, is stated by the prophet to have been changed to foolishness through the country's reliance on unwise rulers; the passage, the text of which is not in order, shows at any rate how the wisdom of Egypt was recognised in Palestine. There are other indications of this, but we need not go into further detail. Egyptian wisdom was looked upon with high respect in Israel, and the probability, not to use a stronger word, of its having influenced such Israelite wisdom as existed as early as the time of Solomon is clearly shown by Gressmann.[1] This is an important point, and must be borne in mind in considering the nature of the relationship between Amen-em-ope's writing and various passages in Proverbs.

But before we come to this it will be well to illustrate the fact of the *diffusion of literary pieces* which became popular, and this for two reasons: first, because it shows the opportunities for borrowing, and secondly, because it helps us to realise that there may be another alternative than that of borrowing to account for similarities and parallels between different writings. For this purpose we propose to give some quotations

[1] In the above-mentioned article, pp. 280 ff.

from an ancient Wisdom book, written originally about the middle of the sixth century B.C. in Babylonia. This book evidently enjoyed great popularity, for it found its way into various countries, where it was translated into the language of the country. Among the places to which it came in course of time was the Jewish colony in Elephantiné, in Egypt (about the latter half of the fifth century B.C.), where it was found translated into Aramaic.[1] It seems also to have been known in Palestine, for there are several passages in Proverbs which point to a knowledge of this writing. It is called 'The Words of Achikar.' We shall add to the quotations from it the passages from Proverbs which show parallelism or similarity.

Achikar 98.	(With) more than watchfulness watch thy mouth, and over what thou hearest harden thy heart ; for a word is (like) a bird, and when he has sent it forth a man does not (recapture it ?).[2]
Prov. iv. 23.	Keep thy heart with all diligence, For out of it are the issues of life.
Achikar 103, 104.	In presence of a king, if (a thing) is commanded thee, it is a burning fire ; hasten, do it ; let it not kindle upon thee and hide (?) thy hands ; for also the word of a king is with wrath of heart : why should wood strive with fire, flesh with a knife, a man with a king ?
Prov. xvi. 14.	The wrath of a king is as messengers of death, But a wise man will pacify it.

[1] See Conybeare, Rendel Harris, and Lewis, *The Story of Ahikar* (1913) ; the same authors in Charles' *Apocrypha*, etc., ii. pp. 715 ff. (1913) ; Cowley, *Jewish Documents of the Time of Ezra*, pp. 81 ff. (1919) ; the quotations given are from Cowley's edition.

[2] A note of interrogation indicates that there is uncertainty about the word.

Achikar 96, 97. My son, do not chatter overmuch till thou reveal every word which comes into thy mind ; for in every place are their eyes and their ears ; but keep watch over thy mouth, and let it not be thy destruction (?).

Prov. xx. 19. He that goeth about as a tale-bearer revealeth secrets ;
Therefore meddle not with him that openeth wide his lips.

Achikar 81, 82. Withhold not thy son from the rod if thou canst not keep him from wickedness. If I smite thee, my son, thou wilt not die ; and if I leave (thee) to thine own heart thou wilt not live.

Prov. xxiii. 13, 14. Withhold not correction from the child,
For if thou beat him with the rod he will not die.
Thou shalt beat him with the rod,
And shalt deliver his soul from Sheol.

Achikar 141. Thy secrets reveal not before thy friends, that thy name be not lightly esteemed before them.

Prov. xxv. 9, 10. Disclose not the secret of another,
Lest he that heareth it revile thee,
And thine infamy turn not away.

Achikar 105, 106. Soft is the tongue of a king, but it breaks the ribs of a dragon.

Prov. xxv. 15. By long forbearing is a judge persuaded,
And a soft tongue breaketh the bone.

Achikar 111. I have lifted sand and carried salt, and there is nothing which is heavier than debt.

Prov. xxvii. 3. A stone is heavy, and the sand weighty,
But a fool's vexation is heavier than them both. (Cp. Ecclus. xxii. 15.)

It is likely enough that a more detailed comparison between the two books would reveal further similarities. So far as the illustrations given are concerned, it will be seen that in some cases the similarity or parallelism is closer than in others ; but in every instance there is a point of attachment of some kind or other. What is, therefore, to be gathered from such a comparison is that, while there may have been borrowing on the part of one or the other writer, there is also the possibility, perhaps probability, that neither borrowed, but that a mass of material had gradually accumulated, largely by means of oral teaching, which had become general property, and which was utilised by different writers, and modified according to individual taste ; in this way the same thought would appear in different settings. Sometimes a parallelism is so striking, *e.g.* between Achikar 81, 82 and Prov. xxiii. 13, 14, that one is almost compelled to postulate borrowing ; but which of the two was the borrower is very difficult, perhaps impossible, to decide. On the other hand, in such a case as Achikar 103, 104 and Prov. xvi. 14 there are distinct similarities, but the differences are far greater ; and this suggests the existence of a common stock lying behind both, of which each writer made such use as seemed good to him. Each case must be considered on its merits. The way in which ' The Words of Achikar ' was spread abroad and translated must be only one instance of what happened with other books.

Now what has been said applies in general to whatever relationship may exist between the ' Teaching of Amen-em-ope ' and the Old Testament books ; but in this case there are some special factors, so that mere generalising will not suffice.

It is probable enough that Amen-em-ope and the compiler of the collections in Proverbs utilised the common floating material of Eastern lands already referred to. This would fully account for the many instances, given in an earlier chapter, of similarity of thought or of word, and of partial parallelism, while at the same time showing substantial differences.

On the other hand, the utilisation of common floating material is not sufficient to account for the close parallelism between certain passages in Amen-em-ope's book and the collection contained in Prov. xxii. 17–xxiii. 14 (or xxiv. 22 if the whole be regarded as one collection). Most of those who have dealt with the subject take for granted that Amen-em-ope's book is the source of the collection in Proverbs. Lange alone asks whether it may not be that Amen-em-ope utilised an older, now lost, Hebrew writing, which was also one of the sources of Proverbs. He asks the question, however, only to reject the hypothesis, and accepts the generally held opinion that the compiler of Proverbs borrowed directly from Amen-em-ope. Nevertheless this suggestion of Lange is worth a little further consideration.[1]

That Prov. xxii. 17–xxiv. 22 is an independent literary piece which has been incorporated by the compiler of Proverbs is generally recognised. When one examines this collection carefully from the point of view of parallelism with Amen-em-ope there are three things to be noted. First, there can be no shadow of doubt regarding the existence of a relationship of some kind between them. Secondly, there is this to be observed : following the Hebrew division there are twenty-five verses in the collection Prov. xxii. 17–xxiii. 14 ; of these, six verses (xxii. 21, 22, 24, 28, 29, xxiii. 8) are very closely paralleled in Amen-em-ope ; seven others (xxii. 23, 26, 27, xxiii. 7, 12–14) are not represented ; in many cases Amen-em-ope is much more expanded than Proverbs ; yet,

[1] The present writer may be permitted to say that a similar idea had suggested itself to him before he had read Lange's book.

with the exception of the seven verses just mentioned, there is a quite obvious relationship, with, at the same time, considerable differences. A third point is this: In the Proverbs collection the verses run, of course, consecutively; but the corresponding passages in Amen-em-ope do not, as a rule, run consecutively; they do in the case of Prov. xxii. 17–19 (= Amen-em-ope i.), and xxiii. 1–3 (= Amen-em-ope xxiii.); but otherwise the parallels with Proverbs xxii. 17–xxiii. 14 occur in ten different chapters of Amen-em-ope. The process is, in the main, reversed in Chaps. X and XXI of Amen-em-ope; here the passages which have parallels in Proverbs run on consecutively in Amen-em-ope, while the corresponding passages in Proverbs are scattered in different parts of the book. While it would be a mistake to lay too much stress on this, especially as so few chapters come into consideration, it is worth drawing attention to, because it seems to point to a difference in the nature of the relationship as between Amen-em-ope and the collection in Prov. xxii. 17–xxiii. 14, on the one hand, and Amen-em-ope and the rest of the Book of Proverbs on the other. If the compiler of Proverbs used Amen-em-ope as the direct source of this collection we should expect to find all the parallel passages running consecutively in each. We should also expect him to have made *more* use of Amen-em-ope in these passages; for in the great majority of cases Amen-em-ope is so much longer than the corresponding Proverbs passage. If the compiler of Proverbs was going to use Amen-em-ope at all for this collection, it is a little bit difficult to understand why he has been so arbitrary in his choice.

If, on the other hand, both utilised some older Hebrew writing, the matter becomes simpler: the compiler of Proverbs made, more or less, a copy of this writing, while Amen-em-ope took a number of its

ideas and elaborated them in his own way, inserting
them into different parts of his book according as he
thought suitable.

Our conclusion, then, so far as the relationship
between the ' Teaching of Amen-em-ope ' and the
Book of Proverbs is concerned, is that the writers of
each were partially indebted to the common stock of
' Wisdom ' material which existed in abundance in
the East.   But, regarding the collection in Prov. xxii.
17–xxiii. 14, the suggestion that both Amen-em-ope
and the compiler of Proverbs made use of an older
Hebrew collection deserves more serious consideration than has yet been given to it.

As to the larger question of the nature of the relationship between Amen-em-ope and other Old Testament books,[1] the outstanding facts to be borne in
mind are, first, the large amount of parallelism in
thought between the two ; and secondly, the uniqueness of Amen-em-ope's book among Egyptian writings.
Here the recognition of the existence of a common
floating material behind both is not sufficient to
account for the facts ; for it can be stated without
fear of contradiction that that floating material did
not contain the conception of God, the ethical teaching,
and the insistence on man's duty to his fellow-creatures
which are found in the Old Testament and in the
' Teaching of Amen-em-ope,' and nowhere else.   Either
we must suppose that some of the Old Testament
writers borrowed from, or at least were influenced by,
Amen-em-ope, or else we must be prepared to acknowledge that Amen-em-ope was acquainted with some
of those Hebrew writings which later became part
of the Old Testament, and was so impressed by their
spirit and teaching that he absorbed them and, perhaps
unconsciously, reproduced them to some extent in

[1] Apart from Proverbs, we are thinking more especially of Psalms
and Deuteronomy.

his own writing. Assuming, as we do, that the Egyptian book was written after the high ethical teaching of the prophets had taken root and fructified among the finer spirits of their nation, it is *à priori* more likely that Amen-em-ope would be influenced by the Old Testament writers than *vice versa*.

So far as ' Wisdom,' pure and simple, is concerned, we would not for a moment deny the influence of Egypt on Israel ; but where it is a question of *religion* and *ethics* we contend that Amen-em-ope and, probably, other Egyptian thinkers of like exalted mentality were more likely to have been influenced by the Hebrew genius than that Israelite religious leaders should have borrowed from Egypt.

Perhaps we have somewhat underestimated the part that Egyptian thought may have played in Israel ; but if so it must be due to the reaction caused by the fact that there has been a tendency at times to overrate Egyptian influence on Israel. We agree, however, entirely with Blackman when he says : ' Just as, on the one hand, specifically native Egyptian contributions to the world's cultural and religious progress penetrated into Palestine and were absorbed into the main stream of Hebrew religious development, so, on the other hand, certain results of the Semitic genius for religion in their turn penetrated into Egypt and contributed to the formulation of what was highest and best in Egyptian religion.' [1]

---

[1] In *The Psalmists*, Introduction, p. xiii.

INDEX OF BIBLICAL PASSAGES

Printed in England at THE BALLANTYNE PRESS
SPOTTISWOODE, BALLANTYNE & CO. LTD.
Colchester, London & Eton.